TRANSCENDING THE *TITANIC*

BEYOND DEATH'S DOOR

TRANSCENDING
THE *TITANIC*

BEYOND DEATH'S DOOR

BY

MICHAEL TYMN

www.whitecrowbooks.com

Transcending the *Titanic*
Beyond Death's Door

Copyright © 2012 by Michael E. Tymn. All rights reserved.

Published and printed in the United States of America and the United Kingdom
by White Crow Books; an imprint of White Crow Productions Ltd.

For information, contact White Crow Books
at P. O. Box 1013 Guildford, GU1 9EJ United Kingdom,
or e-mail to info@whitecrowbooks.com.

Cover Designed by Butterflyeffect
Interior production by essentialworks.co.uk
Interior design by Perseus Design

Paperback ISBN 978-1-908733-02-3
eBook ISBN 978-1-9087331-03-0

Non Fiction / Body, Mind & Spirit / Parapsychology

Published by White Crow Books
www.whitecrowbooks.com

CONTENTS

The whole scene was indescribably pathetic. Many, knowing what had occurred, were in agony of doubt as to their people left behind and as to their own future state. What would it hold for them? Would they be taken to see Him? What would their sentence be? Others were almost mental wrecks. They knew nothing. They seemed to be uninterested in everything, their minds were paralyzed. A strange crew indeed, of human souls waiting their ratings in the new land.

A matter of a few minutes in time only, and here were hundreds of bodies floating in the water – dead – hundreds of souls carried through the air, alive; very much alive, some were. Many, realizing their death had come, were enraged at their own powerlessness to save their valuables. They fought to save what they had on earth prized so much.

– William T. Stead
Titanic Victim

A Different Perspective on the *Titanic* Disaster

As the *Titanic* plunged to the bottom of the Atlantic Ocean, Colonel Archibald Gracie was sucked down with it. However, he somehow managed to surface and survive, and he soon found himself sprawled on an overturned life raft, his clothes waterlogged and his teeth chattering from the icy cold. He noticed that the seaman next to him on the raft had a dry cap and asked him if he could borrow it for just a few minutes to warm his head. "And what wad oi do?" was the curt reply. "Ah, never mind," said Gracie, as he thought "it would make no difference a hundred years hence."

Those hundred years are up this year on April 15 and we might assume that it no longer makes any difference to Colonel Gracie, wherever and however he now exists. But understanding Gracie's ordeal and those of the other 2,222 passengers, including the crew, of the *Titanic*, might make a difference now for some people – those interested in learning from the experiences of others while searching for greater meaning in life's suffering and tragedies.

Basically, the *Titanic* story is about dying and death, a subject many people don't like to think about. "Dying is especially difficult in America," writes Kathleen Dowling Singh, Ph.D., an experienced hospice worker, in her 1998 book, *the Grace in Dying*. "Our cultural blinders to the world of Spirit, to the transpersonal realms, have left us bereft of meaning, struggling alone with the chaos of psychic deconstruction and physical dissolution."

Clearly, science and technology have raced far ahead of our ability to adapt to the changes they have brought about, especially the ability to integrate spiritual ideas and discoveries with those scientific and technological advances. Quite a few people have succumbed to believing in a strictly mechanistic universe, one devoid of a spiritual world.

It has been my observation that most of those people – the "scientific fundamentalists" – are reacting against the superstitions of orthodox religion, not really grasping the difference between the views of orthodoxy and the spirituality which many true seekers of truth have come to recognize. Others cling to the dogma and doctrine of various religions, refusing to accept more progressive and enlightened spiritual views.

This book is not quite like other books about the *Titanic*. As the title suggests, it is an attempt to explore the more transcendental aspects of the *Titanic* story – those suggesting a non-mechanistic universe. The subjects include premonitions, apparitions, out-of-body experiences, telepathic communication among the living, and after-death communication, many related to the *Titanic* passengers, others offered in support of the *Titanic* phenomena. Key among the passengers is William T. Stead, a British journalist. Although much has been written about Stead's spiritual pursuits and experiences, very little of it has been discussed in other books about the disaster. Thus, I believe that the book is somewhat unique in this respect.

Unlike other books about the *Titanic*, this one does not go into a lot of detail about the ship and its passengers. However, Chapter One offers a general overview of what took place between the time the ship hit an iceberg and the time the surviving passengers were rescued. Some general facts and a timeline follow.

Facts & Figures

The *Titanic*, the largest passenger steamship in the world at the time, was on its maiden voyage from Southampton, England to New York City, in the northwest Atlantic Ocean, when it hit an iceberg at approximately 11:40 p.m. on April 14, 1912. It went to its watery grave at approximately 2:20 a.m. on April 15. Of the 2,223 passengers and crew aboard, 1,517 perished, many of them from hypothermia resulting from the 28 degrees ocean cold.

After undergoing sea trials on April 2, 1912, the ship, owned by White Star Line and constructed at the Harland and Wolff shipyard in Belfast, Ireland, sailed from Southampton on the southern coast of England on April 10, arriving in Cherbourg, France 90 minutes later, departing Cherbourgh at 8:10 p.m. the same day, then arriving at Queenstown in County Cork, Ireland at 11:30 a.m. It departed there for New York City at 1:40 p.m. April 11.

Of the 2,223 passengers and crew, 1,324 were paying passengers and 899 were crew members. Only 706 survived. The high casualty rate was due, in great part, to the fact that the ship carried lifeboats with a capacity of only 1,178. Some of the lifeboats left with less than capacity because most of the passengers and crew did not believe the ship could sink.

Timeline

April 10, 1912 – Departs Southampton, England

April 14 – 11:40 p.m., Hits iceberg

April 15 – 12:15 a.m., Women are urged to head for lifeboats

12:20 a.m., *Carpathia* receives C.Q.D. (S.O.S) message from *Titanic*

12:45 a.m., First lifeboat lowered

1:10 a.m., First explosion

1:30 a.m., Word passed that ship appears doomed

1:55 a.m., Last standard-sized lifeboat lowered

2:00 a.m., Another explosion, lights go out

2:05 a.m., Entire bow now underwater

2:05 a.m., Last Englehardt boat (small lifeboat) launched

2:10 a.m., Ship begins breaking apart

2:15 a.m., With front part of ship broken away and headed for the bottom, the stern rises to a perpendicular position

2:20 a.m., Stern of the ship sinks

4:10 a.m., *Carpathia* arrives

4:30 a.m., *Carpathia* finishes boarding first lifeboat

8:30 a.m., *Carpathia* finishes boarding all lifeboats

April 18 – *Carpathia* arrives in New York.

Understanding Our Fascination with the *Titanic*

On April 27, 1865, a boiler explosion on the *Santana*, a Mississippi River steamboat, resulted in the deaths of 1,547 people, most of them Union soldiers returning home at the end of the United States Civil War. Although the death toll of the *Santana* exceeds the 1,517 reported for the RMS *Titanic*, it seems safe to say that the *Santana* is all but forgotten, while the story of the *Titanic* continues to fascinate millions.

Might we attribute the difference to the fact that the *Titanic* disaster happened "only" 100 years ago, while that of the Santana was 147 years ago? No, if we could go back 47 years in time to the year 1965, it is highly unlikely that many people then would have been able to identify the *Santana*. Moreover, the great San Francisco earthquake and fire of 1906, took place just six years before the *Titanic* sinking and involved an estimated 3,000 deaths, twice as many as the *Titanic*, and yet that terrible event does not stir up nearly as much emotion and interest as that of the *Titanic*. Much more recent than the *Titanic*, the "Great Smog" of London, took an estimated 4,000 lives in 1952. But how many people remember it? Thus, it does not appear that time answers the question of why the *Titanic* is so remembered today.

In terms of lives lost in maritime disasters, the *Titanic* falls far short of the estimated 4,000 killed when the *Dona Paz*, a passenger ferry, collided with an oil tanker off Mindoro Island, south of Manila, Philippines during 1987. The reason the *Dona Paz* is not as well remembered, at least in the Western world, is likely a result of its location and limited media attention in Western countries.

No doubt the many movies made of the *Titanic* disaster, especially the 1997 epic film, play a big part in our continuing knowledge of and interest in the *Titanic* story, but that only leads to the question of why movie makers find it so much more interesting than other disasters. In fact, there have been at least eight movies about the *Titanic*, eight more in which the *Titanic* has been featured, nine movies inspired by the *Titanic*, and at least seven television documentaries reporting on it.

Clearly, the common denominator of the interest and intrigue in all disasters is death and its before and after concomitants, dying, and surviving in another realm of existence. Who, after attaining the age or reason, has not thought about how he will die or when she will die or if he will continue to exist after he dies? Such thoughts may be only fleeting in our younger years, but they usually become more frequent and affect the psyche in a much more profound way as we age and approach death's door.

"What we most dread," wrote Belgian Maurice Maeterlinck, the 1911 Nobel Prize winner in literature, "is the awful struggle at the end and especially the last, terrible second of rupture which we shall perhaps see approaching during long hours of helplessness and which suddenly hurls us, naked, disarmed, abandoned by all and stripped of everything, into an unknown that is the home of the only invisible terrors which the soul of man has every felt." As Maeterlinck saw it, the roots of our fears were placed in our hearts by religions, by then obsolete.

"The idea of death, the fear of it, haunts the human mind like nothing else," wrote anthropologist Ernest Becker in his 1974 Pulitzer prize-winning book, *The Denial of Death*. Becker added that man's deepest need is to be free of the anxiety of death and annihilation, and explained that to free oneself of death anxiety, nearly everyone chooses the path of repression. That is, we bury the anxiety deep in the subconscious while we busy ourselves with our lives and seek a mundane security that we expect to continue indefinitely. To put it another way, we escape from our fear of death by becoming Philistines and not thinking about it.

"Although there are undoubtedly special circumstances in which some individuals either welcome their own cessation or are essentially indifferent to it, for almost everybody the heightened probability of death constitutes the most dire threat possible," wrote Edwin S. Shneidman, professor of medical psychology at UCLA and a former chief of the National Institute of Mental Health Center for Studies of Suicide Prevention, in his 1973 book, *Deaths of Man*.

Well before Becker and Shneidman, pioneering psychiatrists Sigmund Freud, Carl Jung, and William James recognized that the "denial of death" or death anxiety is at the core of human behavior. However, while Freud had adopted a materialistic outlook and believed that death meant extinction, both Jung and James remained agnostic on the issue of survival. Freud believed that humans would be better off if they simply opened themselves to death and accepted it as annihilation, but Jung and James believed that life could be lived to the fullest only by embracing the idea of life after death, even if untrue. "Death is indeed a fearful piece of brutality," Jung offered. "There is no sense in pretending otherwise. It is brutal not only as a physical event, but far more so psychically."

Freud, Jung, James, and Becker all recognized a need for humans to deal with death by allowing it to surface from the subconscious to the conscious to some degree, if not completely. But their hopes in this regard have been little realized. Most humans allow the reality of death to surface only when dealing with unreality – when they escape into the fiction, non-fiction, or semi-fiction of books and movies. "The cinema....like the detective story makes it possible to experience without danger all the excitement, passion, and desirousness which must be repressed in a humanitarian order of life," Jung explained.

Not everyone, however, is able to successfully repress his or her death anxiety. Leo Tolstoy, the brilliant Russian author, was one such person. Although reared in the Greek Orthodox Church, Tolstoy, gradually lost his faith, and by age 50 was in despair at not being able to find any meaning in life. He wrote:

> The mental state in which I then was seemed to me summed up in the following: my life was a foolish and wicked joke played upon me by I knew not whom. Not withstanding my rejection of the idea of a creator, that of a being who thus wickedly and foolishly made a joke of me seemed to me the most natural of all conclusions, and the one that threw the most light upon my darkness. I instinctively reasoned that this being, wherever he might be, was one who was even then diverting himself at my expense, as he watched me, after from thirty to forty years of a life of study and development, of mental and bodily growth, with all my powers matured and having reached the point at which life as a whole should be best understood, standing like a fool with but with one thing clear to me, that there was nothing in

life, that there never was anything, and never will be. "To him I must seem ridiculous but was there, or was there not, such a being?" Neither way could I feel it helped me. I could not attribute reasonable motive to any single act, much less to my whole life. I was only astonished that this had not occurred to me before, from premises, which had so long been known. Illness and death would come (indeed they had come), if not today, then tomorrow, to those whom I loved, to myself, and nothing would remain but stench and worms. All my acts, whatever I did, would sooner or later be forgotten, and I myself am nowhere. Why, then, busy one's self with anything? How could men see this and live? It is possible to live only as long as life intoxicates us; as soon as we are sober again we see that it is all a delusion, and a stupid one! In this, indeed, there is nothing either ludicrous or amusing; it is only cruel and absurd.

The *Titanic* story offers us the opportunity to examine death in a safe haven with the added bonus that, unlike most stories involving death, the parties actually have time to contemplate theirs death, some to escape, some to succumb. More than any other modern story, the *Titanic* might be viewed as a microcosm of life, a "community" isolated in the vast reaches of the ocean, one offering wealth and poverty, the opulence of first class and the ordinariness of steerage class, with a middle or second class in between. Every type of emotion, mindset, virtue and vice is represented – love and fear, hope and despair, bravery and cowardice, arrogance and humbleness, pomp and shame, selfishness and brotherhood. To accent it all, the iceberg impacted by the leviathan was reported as being a rare black berg looming high over the vessel, as if a giant evil predator. More than anything though, the *Titanic* story represents the struggle between man's inner self and outer self, a struggle which many people are interested in but prefer to avoid except in books or movies. .

One must also consider the era in which the tragedy took place. It was a time when science was conquering religion and the educated class had not yet been able to reconcile its former religious beliefs with the truths provided by science. Beginning in 1859, Darwinism accelerated the underlying *Weltschmerz* (despair). More and more educated people began to see life as a march toward an abyss of nothingness, toward extinction, toward obliteration. Biological evolution had, for many, nullified God, and few seemed to be able to grasp an afterlife without

God; thus, it was also dismissed. Suddenly, life had no meaning beyond what one could leave behind for his descendants or future generations, but even this worthy goal left the reasoning man wondering to what end the progeny or to which generation full fruition.

"Never, perhaps, did man's spiritual satisfaction bear a smaller proportion to his needs," wrote Cambridge scholar and poet Frederic W. H. Myers, referring to the 1870s. "The old-world sustenance, however earnestly administered, [was] too unsubstantial for the modern cravings. And thus through our civilized societies two conflicting currents [ran]. On the one hand, health, intelligence, morality – all such boons as the steady progress of planetary evolution can win for the man – [were] being achieved in increasing measure. On the other hand this very sanity, this very prosperity, [brought out] in stronger relief the underlying *Weltschmerz*, the decline of any real belief in the dignity, the meaning, the endlessness of life."

Myers said that there were many who readily accepted the limitations of the new view and who were willing to let earthly activities gradually dissipate and obscure the larger hope, but others could not be satisfied. "They rather resemble children who are growing too old for their games – whose amusement sinks into indifference and discontent for which the fitting remedy is an initiation into the serious work of men."

William James called it "soul sickness" and admitted that he, too, suffered from it, even considering suicide around the time he received his M.D. degree from Harvard University. While this soul sickness seems to have peaked around 1875, little progress had been made in overcoming the affliction by 1912, when the *Titanic* dove to its watery grave. Materialism had become the new philosophy and when carried too far it came to be hedonism, the motto for which is "eat, drink, and be merry, for tomorrow we die," an attitude seemingly depicted on the *Titanic*, at least among the first class passengers.

Writing in the March 1912 issue of the Journal of the American Society for Psychical Research, the month before the *Titanic* went down, psychologist James H. Hyslop, a former professor of logic and ethics at Columbia University, discussed the continuing decline in man's belief in life after death, stating:

The belief in immortality had been so bound up with a large number of dogmas that had to succumb to the revival of science that it too was carried away with them. Christianity had cut the Gordian knot of materialism by denying the eternity of matter and making it an ephemeral product of divine creation. But the indestructibility of matter and the conservation of force played havoc with this belief and personality became, not the initiating cause of things, but their phenomenon or function. Ever since, the idea of survival after bodily death has been a declining doctrine. The hypothesis of evolution, following the central significance of the indestructibility of matter and the conservation of energy, displaced the theory of special creation and established the struggle for existence as the model of human conduct. There was no survival of personality to mitigate the cruelties of nature and society. All the achievements of the individual in the pursuit of his ideals ended with bodily death and the pall of despair hung over every hope that man endeavored to cherish. He was not satisfied with his sensuous life and the physical and economic system did not make possible, in this life, the realization of the inner ideals that he either felt or was told to value above all else. He saw only the chance to share in a struggle where superior wit obtained the rewards and virtue was left to those anemic souls that could be elbowed out of the way by methods that only come short of murder and violent asphyxiation. In this system the individual counts for nothing. He is a sacrifice to the race, forgetting that the race is nothing but the individual multiplied.

Whether entirely fiction or not is unclear, but in a 1986 book titled *The Secret Conan Doyle Correspondence*, author Leslie Vernet Harper quotes her father Samuel Harper, supposedly a *Titanic* survivor though not listed on the passenger manifest, as seeing the *Titanic* as a symbol of the times and its fate as a foreboding cosmic message: "Words are inadequate to convey the awesome impact of that enormous floating palace – the epitome in every respect of the biggest and most lavish the Western world had to offer in material luxury. In an era idolatrously committed to the proposition that science unquestionably could overcome every obstacle standing between mankind and Utopia, the *Titanic* was living, dynamic proof of this utopian ideal."

As Harper further viewed it, the disaster changed the world in unfathomably deep ways. "The death of the *Titanic* tipped the scales in favor of those who, like historian Oswald Spengler, looked for the 'going under of the West.' And it fatally shook the confidence of the optimists, those who thought it possible to resolve mankind's dilemma through science without any moral improvement in man himself...Now, the sinking of the 'unsinkable' *Titanic* having demonstrated the inadequacy of the science alternative, there remained only what a majority viewed as unworkable – the need for mankind to live the Christian ideal."

But there was hardly time to fully integrate the lessons of the *Titanic* into our psyches before the outbreak of a much greater tragedy in terms of loss of life, World War I. This horrible event made man search even more deeply for his lost soul, and while many were successful in their search, peace time brought about renewed materialism and hedonism and the newfound soul was again lost.

And so it has continued until today – a great tragedy, such as that of September 11, 2001, brings a temporary search for the soul, but it is quickly forgotten in man's quest for comfort through technical and scientific advancement.

"We have measured the earth, the stars, and the depths of the seas; we have discovered riverbeds and mountains on the moon," wrote Tolstoy. "We have built clever machines, and every day we discover something new ... But something, some most important thing, is missing, and we do not know exactly what. We feel bad because we know lots of unnecessary things but do not know the most important — ourselves."

Thus viewed, the *Titanic* story may represent a search for ourselves.

ONE

FACING DEATH ON THE HIGH SEAS

I think we all learnt many things that night about the bogey called "fear," and how the facing of it is much less than the dread of it.
— **Lawrence Beesley**
Titanic survivor

Four survivors of the *Titanic* reported seeing William Thomas Stead at various places in the 2 hours and 40 minutes that elapsed between the time the floating palace hit an iceberg and the time it made its plunge to the bottom of the North Atlantic. All of them told of a very composed and calm man, one prepared to meet his death with dignified expectation.

Frederick Seward, a 34-year-old New York lawyer, said that Stead was one of the few on deck when the iceberg was impacted. "I saw him soon after and [I] was thoroughly scared, but he preserved the most beautiful composure," Seward, who boarded lifeboat 7, recalled.

Andrew Cunningham, a 35-year-old English cabin steward serving Stead and several other passengers, recalled that Stead had not been feeling well all day and had supper in his room. "I did not see him again until after the accident," Cunningham related. "Then I went to see all my passengers. He had gone on deck but soon came back. I said, 'Mr. Stead, you'll have to put on your life-belt.' He said, 'Cunningham, what is that for?' I said, 'You may need it.' I put the belt over his head. We bade each other goodbye, and that was the last I saw him."

Racing through the first-class smoking room on his way to lifeboat 9, George Kemish, a 24-year-old ship's fireman and stoker, observed

Stead sitting alone there while reading, as if he had planned to stay there, whatever happened.

Juanita Parrish Shelley, a 25-year-old second-class passenger from Montana who was traveling with her mother, saw Stead assisting women and children into the lifeboats. "Your beloved Chief," Shelley later wrote to Edith Harper, Stead's loyal secretary and biographer, "together with Mr. and Mrs. (Isidor) Strauss, attracted attention even in that awful hour, on account of their superhuman composure and divine work. When we, the last lifeboat, left, and they could do no more, he stood alone, at the edge of the deck, near the stern, in silence and what seemed to me a prayerful attitude, or one of profound meditation. You ask if he wore a life-belt. Alas! No, they were too scarce. My last glimpse of the *Titanic* showed him standing in the same attitude and place."

Certainly, Stead was not the only victim of the *Titanic* to face death with relative composure and calmness, although in many cases it may not have been easy to distinguish between Stead's "dignified expectation" and the nihilist's "stoic resignation." One likely would have to search the eyes for hope or despair in order to discern the difference. In either case, the person might be described as brave, courageous, or, if aiding others to his own detriment, as heroic. Indeed, the stoic might be considered more brave or more courageous, though more pathetic, since he does not have the support of hope and expectation.

A third alternative in facing death is "controlled trembling," in which the person's inner turmoil is for the most part held in check so that it does not negatively affect or carry over to others. This individual is likely in despair with at least a modicum of hope. The fourth, and least acceptable, alternative is "uncontrolled trembling" or "panic," in which the person is in complete despair and acts with total disregard for others in an attempt to save himself.

"The way in which a man accepts his fate and all the suffering it entails, the way in which he takes up his cross, gives him ample opportunity – even under the most difficult circumstances – to add a deeper meaning to his life," wrote Viktor E. Frankl in *Man's Search for Meaning.* "It may remain brave, dignified and unselfish. Or in the bitter fight for self-preservation he may forget his human dignity and become no more than an animal. Here lies the chance for a man either to make use of or to forgo the opportunities of attaining the moral values that a difficult situation may afford him. And this decides whether he is worthy of his suffering or not."

It is difficult to measure the fear factor on the *Titanic* during the first two hours following the collision, because the preponderance of testimony suggests that very few of the passengers really believed that the "unsinkable" ship would sink. "One of the most remarkable features of this horrible affair is the length of time that elapsed after the collision before the seriousness of the situation dawned on the passengers," Robert W. Daniel, a 27-year-old first-class passenger from Philadelphia, testified. "The officers assured everybody that there was no danger, and we all had such confidence in the *Titanic* that it didn't occur to anybody that she might sink."

Daniel jumped into the ocean before the ship went down and was picked up by one of the lifeboats. He said that "men fought and bit and struck one another like madmen," referring to those in the water attempting to save themselves. He was reportedly picked up naked with wounds about his face, and then nearly died from the exposure to the cold before he was rescued.

Even when, an hour after the accident, the captain ordered the lifeboats to be lowered, the severity of the situation was not realized by most. It was seen as a precautionary measure. "No one, apparently, thought there was any danger," Lady Duff-Gordon (Lucy Christiana), the wife of Sir Cosmo Edmund Duff-Gordon, was quoted in the April 19 issue of the *Denver Post*. "We watched a number of women and children and some men going into the lifeboats. At last one of the officers came to me and said, 'Lady Gordon, you had better go into one of the lifeboats.' I said to my husband, 'Well, we might as well take the boat, although I think it will be only a little pleasure excursion until morning.'"

Lady Gordon also recalled that a number of other passengers, mostly men, were standing nearby and laughed at those boarding the lifeboats, saying that the ship can't sink and they would "get your death of cold" out there on the ice. That was around 1 a.m., roughly an hour and 20 minutes after the collision and an hour and 20 minutes before the sinking.

"The whole forward part of the great liner dropped down under the waves," Lady Gordon gave her account of the final moments. "The stern rose a hundred feet almost perpendicularly. The screaming was agonizing. I never heard such a continued chorus of utter despair and agony. The great power of the *Titanic* slowly sank as though a great hand was pushing it gently down under the waves. As it went, the screaming of the poor souls left on board seemed to grow louder. It took the *Titanic* perhaps two minutes to sink after the last explosion.

It went down slowly without a ripple. We had heard of the danger of suction when one of these great liners sinks. There was no such thing about the sinking of the *Titanic*. The amazing part of it all to me as I sat there in the boat looking at this monster being destroyed was that it all could be accomplished so gently. Then began the real agonies of the night. Up to that time no one in our boat, and I imagine no one on any of the other boats, had really thought that the *Titanic* was going to sink. For a moment an awful silence seemed to hang over all, and then from the water all about where the *Titanic* had been arose a bedlam of shrieks and cries. There were men and women clinging to the bits of wreckage in the icy water. It was at least an hour before the last shrieks died out. I remember the very last cry was that a man had been calling loudly: 'My God! My God!' He cried monotonously in a dull, hopeless way. For an entire hour there had been an awful chorus of shrieks, gradually dying into a hopeless moan until this last cry that I speak of. Then all was silent."

Only 12 people were in the lifeboat occupied by Sir Cosmo and Lady Duff-Gordon, even though it had a capacity of 40. Seven of those 12 were crew members. It was reported by crew member Charles Hendrickson that Lady Gordon objected to the lifeboat returning to pick up those in the water after the ship went down for fear that the boat would be swamped. Several of the men agreed and Charles Henry Stengel, another first-class passenger, suggested that they should head for a light that could be seen in the distance (possibly the S.S. *Californian*, which did not respond to the distress signals). Thus, they rowed away while hundreds were left freezing to death in the water.

It was also claimed that Sir Cosmo offered the crew members money not to go back, but when he was called to answer this claim before a British inquiry board, he explained that one of the crew complained that he would never be paid by the White Star Line for his limited voyage, and so he offered five pounds to each crew member and kept his promise after boarding the *Carpathia*, the ship that rescued them. Lady Gordon also appeared before the board and denied that she heard any of the cries of those drowning and further denied that she objected to going back to pick them up.

Caroline Bonnell, a 30-year-old first-class passenger from Youngstown, Ohio, also underestimated the seriousness of the situation. She and her cousin, Mary Wick, were half asleep in their bunks when they felt the collision. They went out to the deck, saw nothing to alarm them, and then were preparing to return to their cabin when an officer told them to go below and put on their lifebelts. "We went down at once and told my aunt and uncle, Mr. and Mrs. George Wick, what we had been told," Bonnell was quoted in the April 19 issue of the *Christian Science Monitor*. "Uncle George just laughed at us. 'Why, that's nonsense, girls,' he said. 'This boat is all right. She's going along nicely. She just got a glancing blow, I guess.' That's the way every one seemed to think and we went into our stateroom, but in a minute or so an officer knocked at the door and told us to go up on the 'A' deck. He said there was really no danger and that it was just a precautionary measure. When we got on the deck uncle and aunt were there and I went down again to another part of the steamer and got my Aunt Elizabeth. When I got back with her, there were crowds of people standing all around. Nobody seemed very excited; every one was talking and it seemed to be the general idea that we would soon be ordered back to bed. Just then an officer came up to us and said we should go up to the next deck – the boat deck. By that time nearly every one was up. Mrs. John Jacob Astor was there sitting in a steamer chair. Her husband, Colonel Astor, was beside her and her maid was helping her to finish her dressing. There was no confusion here even yet, although we noticed that the boat was beginning to list to starboard."

Lawrence Beesley, a 34-year-old teacher and second class passenger who later wrote a book about his experience and observations, described an initial calmness or lack of panic. "The fact is that the sense of fear came to the passengers very slowly – a result of the absence of any signs of danger and the peaceful night – and as it became evident gradually that there was serious damage to the ship, the fear that came with the knowledge was largely destroyed as it came. There was no sudden overwhelming sense of danger that passed through thought so quickly that it was difficult to catch up and grapple with it – no need for the warning to 'be not afraid of sudden fear,' such as might have been present had we collided head-on with a crash and a shock that flung everyone out of his bunk to the floor. Everyone had time to give each condition of danger attention as it came along, and the result of their judgment was as if they had said: 'Well, here is this thing to be faced, and we must see it through as quietly as we can.' Quietness and self-control were undoubtedly the two qualities most expressed." However, Beesley was a mile or so away from the ship when it went down and was in no position to judge the mental states of those left behind during final hour.

Although the captain had given the order "women and children only" many men, including Beesley were able to board the lifeboats.

Beesley explained that lifeboat 13 was only about half full when he heard the cry, "Any more ladies?" The call was repeated twice with no response before one of the crew looked at him and told him to jump in. After he was in the boat, three more ladies and one man showed up and boarded. "We rowed away from her in the quietness of the night, hoping and praying with all our hearts that she would sink no more and the day would find her still in the same position as she was then," Beesley continued, stressing that the belief remained strong that the *Titanic* could not sink and it was only a matter of time before another ship showed up and took everyone aboard. "Husbands expected to follow their wives and join them either in New York or by transfer in mid-ocean from steamer to steamer...It is not any wonder, then, that many elected to remain, deliberately choosing the deck of the *Titanic* to a place in the lifeboat. And yet the boats had to go down, and so at first they were half full; this is the real explanation of why they were not as fully loaded as the later ones."

While some of the press and the public initially looked with suspicion upon all of the 338 men saved, it became clear that some of them were picked up from the ocean, including from an overturned raft, while others, like Beesley, were invited to get in when no other women or children were around to fill the lifeboat, and still others were commissioned by those in charge to row the boats.

The person most suspect of being a coward was J. Bruce Ismay, the 49-year-old president of the International Mercantile Marine, owners of White Star Line. There were conflicting reports as to whether he was in of the first lifeboats to leave or the last and what prompted him to get in the boat in the first place. Mary Louise Smith, the 18-year-old wife of Lucien Smith, claimed that Ismay was escorted by seamen into the lifeboat she occupied, one of the first to leave. She further alleged that Captain Smith was standing nearby and that she implored him to let her husband in the boat, but he refused, even though there were only about 20 people in the boat, which had a capacity of fifty to sixty. However, Thomas Cardeza, a 36-year-old "gentleman" and first-class passenger from Germantown, Pennsylvania, testified that Ismay at first refused to enter the lifeboat, one of the last to leave, and was urged by several women to get in the boat, saying that they would feel safer if he were in it. He finally consented.

Quartermaster George Rowe, in charge of the last boat to leave the port side, at approximately 1:40 a.m., about 40 minutes before the ship foundered, testified before the American Court of Inquiry that Ismay got in his boat only after it was clear that no one else was around to board it. However, he heard no one ask Ismay to get in the boat. In testifying before the British Court of Inquiry, Ismay stated that the boat was ready to be lowered and since no one else was around on that side of the ship, he got in.

One member of the inquiry court questioned Ismay as to his duty to search for other people to fill the boats. However, board members agreed that if there were such a duty it was a moral duty and that such duties were not within the jurisdiction of the board. In Ismay's defense, Sir Robert Finlay, counsel for White Star Company, argued that there was no duty on his part to go down with the ship, as the captain did. "He did all he did to help the women and the children. It was only when the boat was being lowered that he got into it. He violated no point of honor, and if he had thrown his life away in the manner now suggested it would be said he did it because he was conscious he could not face his inquiry and so he had lost his life."

Some women apparently remained on the ship because the risk of boarding a lifeboat seemed greater than that of staying on the ship. "Many believed it was safer to stay on board the big liner even wounded as she was, than to trust themselves to the boats," Albert Smith, a ship's steward, was quoted. The lifeboats hung 70-75 feet above the ocean as crew members struggled to lower them in jolts and jerks. "Our lifeboat, with thirty-six in it, began lowering to the sea," Elizabeth Shutes, a 40-year-old first-class passenger and governess to passenger Margaret Graham, recounted. "This was done amid the greatest confusion. Rough seamen all giving different orders. No officer aboard. As only one side of the ropes worked, the lifeboat at one time was in such a position that it seemed we must capsize in mid-air. At last the ropes worked together, and we drew nearer and nearer the black, oily water." Shutes added that there was some reluctance to row away from the ship, as it felt much safer being near it, so certain they were that it would not sink.

There were reports of men rushing the life boats, jumping in them as they were being lowered, and even stowing away in them under cover. "Some men came and tried to rush the boat," crew member Joseph Scarrot, in charge of lifeboat 14, testified. "They were foreigners and could not understand the orders I gave them, but I managed to keep them away. I had to use some persuasion with a boat tiller. One man jumped in twice and I had to throw him out the third time."

Fifth Officer H. G. Lowe reported that one passenger, an Italian, boarded one of the boats dressed like a woman, with a shawl over his head. As the boat was being lowered he noted a lot of passengers along the rails "glaring more of less like wild beasts, ready to spring." He said he fired three warning shots and did not hit anybody.

Annie May Stengel, a 43-year-old first-class passenger whose husband, Charles, escaped the ship in a later lifeboat, reported that four men jumped into her lifeboat as it was being lowered, one of them Dr. Henry Frauenthal, a New York City physician, who landed on her and knocked her unconscious.

Ella White, a 55-year-old first-class passenger, said that some stewards boarded her lifeboat under the pretense of being oarsmen, but then didn't know enough about rowing to put the oar in the oarlock. "We were the second boat (No. 8) that got away from the ship and we saw nothing that happened after that," she was quoted. "We were not near enough. We heard the yells of the passengers as they went down, but we saw none of the harrowing part of it. The women in our boat all rowed – every one of them. Miss Young rowed every minute. The men (the stewards) did not know the first thing about it and could not row."

But the stories of bravery or simple resignation in the face of fear far outnumber those of cowardice. One of the most celebrated cases of bravery reported by the press immediately following the tragedy was that of Rosalie Straus, the 63-year-old wife of New York department store magnate Isidor Straus. She was observed about to enter a lifeboat when she reversed directions and was overhead to say to her husband, "We have lived together for many years, where you go, I go." Witnesses then saw the two settle in deck chairs. An April 17 article in the *San Francisco Chronicle*, quoted Mrs. Samuel Bessinger, a relative, as saying that Mrs. Straus may not have realized the gravity of the situation, but even if she had, she doubted that she would have left her husband, so devoted she was.

Major Archie Butt, a 46-year-old aide to President William Howard Taft, was praised by several surviving passengers. "I questioned those of the survivors who were in a condition to talk, and from them I learned that Butt, when the *Titanic* struck, took his position with the officers and from the moment the order to man the lifeboats was given until the last one was dropped from the sea, he aided in the maintenance of discipline and the placing of the women and children in the boats," wrote Captain Charles Crain, a passenger on the *Carpathia*. "Butt, I was told, was as cool as the iceberg that had doomed the ship, and not once did he lose control of himself. In the presence of death he was the same gallant, courteous officer that the American people had learned to know so well as a result of his constant attendance upon President Taft.

"There was never any chance of Butt getting into any of those lifeboats. He knew his time was at hand, and he was ready to meet it as a man should, and I and all of the others who cherish his memory are glad that he faced the situation that way, which was the only possible way a man of his caliber could face it."

Benjamin Guggenheim, the millionaire smelter magnate, asked John Johnson, his room steward, to give Mrs. Guggenheim a message if he (Johnson) survived, which he did. "Tell her that I played the game straight and that no woman was left on board this ship because Benjamin Guggenheim was a coward. Tell her that my last thoughts were of her and the girls."

Multi-millionaire John Jacob Astor, 47, is said to have initially ridiculed the idea of leaving the ship in lifeboats, saying that the solid decks of the *Titanic* were safer than a small lifeboat. However, by 1:45 a.m. he had changed his mind and helped his 18-year-old wife, Madeleine, board the last lifeboat. He asked Second Officer Charles Lightoller if he could also board and was told that no men were allowed. Astor then stood back and reportedly stood alone as others tried to free the remaining collapsible boat.

The ship's band, or orchestra, was praised by all surviving passengers. Beesley recalled that they began playing around 12:40 a.m., an hour after the collision, and continued until after 2 a.m. "Many brave things were done that night, but none more brave than by those few men playing minute after minute as the ship settled quietly lower and lower in the sea and the sea rose higher and higher to where they stood; the music they played serving alike as their own immortal requiem and their right to be recorded on the rolls of undying fame."

While it was generally reported that "Nearer My God to Thee" was one of the selections, even the final one, many passengers, including Colonel Archibald Gracie, a 53-year-old Washington, D.C. resident, did not think so, and said it would have been a tactless warning of immediate death to all and would likely have created a panic. Gracie also wrote a book about the sinking and interviewed many passengers, finding only two who remembered hearing the hymn played.

Whatever the hymn, Hilda Slater, a passenger in the last lifeboat to leave the ship, said that the music did much to keep up the spirits of everyone and probably served considerably in the efforts of the officers to prevent panic.

Interestingly, a 2004 article posted at *Encyclopedia Titanica,* an Internet site, by Senan Molony suggests that the playing of the music contributed to the death toll by creating "a mood of conviviality, of unity, of optimism," thus giving "auditory assurance that all was well." Molony argues that more passengers would have boarded the lifeboats had they not been lulled into a false sense of security.

A mistake or not, those seven orchestra members, under the direction of Wallace Hartley, deserve admiration, and they serve as an example as to how to die with grace.

Another case of bravery involved Edith Evans, a 36-year-old New York City resident. Colonel Gracie encountered Evans and Caroline Lane Brown, a 59-year-old Belmont, Massachusetts resident, in a passageway and rushed them to the last lifeboat. Gracie was not allowed to advance up to the boats, but was later told by Brown what happened. Miss Evans led the way, Brown told him, as they neared the rail where the lifeboat was loading. Evans insisted on Brown going first, stating, "You go first. You are married and have children." But when Evans attempted to follow, she was unable to do so, apparently because the boat was already being lowered and the gap between the deck and the boat was by then too great. Evans yelled to Brown that she would go on a later boat. She then ran away and was never seen again.

Gracie was one of the last, if not the last, survivor to leave the ship. About 10 minutes before the ship went down, he and several others struggled to launch a collapsible life raft, referred to as an Englehardt boat. Just as they broke it free, they were hit by a giant wave, apparently from one of the ship's four funnels collapsing and falling. "The big wave carried the boat off," Gracie related. "I had hold of an oarlock and I went off with it. The next I knew I was in the boat. But that was not all. I was in the boat and the boat was upside down and I was under it….How I got out from under the boat I do not know, but I felt a breath at last."

While the "big wave" carried Gracie to safety, Gracie's friend, Clinch Smith, and others, possibly William Stead included, were knocked about and did not survive it. As Gracie saw it, they were knocked against the walls of the officers' quarters and other appurtenances of the ship on the boat deck and rendered unconscious. "My holding on to the iron railing just when I did prevented my being knocked unconscious," Gracie continued his survival story. "I pulled myself over on the roof on my stomach, but before I could get to my feet I was in a whirlpool of water, swirling round and round…Down, down, I went. It seemed a great distance. There was a very noticeable pressure upon my ears, though there must have been plenty of air that the ship carried down with it. When under water I retained, as it appears, a sense of general direction, and, as soon as I could do so, swam away from the starboard side of the ship, as I knew my life depended upon it."

Gracie concluded that the life preserver he wore prevented him from being drawn down by suction to a greater depth. He could not judge how long he was under water, but it "seemed an interminable time until I could scarcely stand it any longer." He recalled thinking that he wanted to convey the news of how he died to his loved ones at home. It was at this point that he somehow telepathically connected with his wife, as discussed in Chapter Two.

When he finally surfaced, he grabbed on to a piece of floating debris and noticed that the ship was gone. "The agonizing cries of death from over a thousand throats, the wails and groans of the suffering, the shrieks of the terror-stricken and the awful gaspings for breath of those in the last throes of drowning, none of us will ever forget to our dying days, "Help! Help! Boat ahoy! Boat ahoy!" and "My God! My God!" were the heartrending cries and shrieks of men, which floated to us over the surface of the dark waters continuously for the next hour, but as the time went on, growing weaker and weaker until they died out entirely."

Gracie then came upon the same Englehardt boat he had helped launch. It was upturned and more than a dozen men were on it. "When I reached the side of the boat I met with a doubtful reception, and, as no extending hand was held out to me, I grabbed, by the muscle of the left arm, a young member of the crew nearest and facing me. At the same time, I threw my right leg over the boat astraddle, pulling myself aboard, with a friendly lift to my foot given someone astern as I assumed a reclining position with them on the bottom of the capsized boat." He was soon joined by a dozen or more other swimmers. Strangely, Gracie recalled, he did not feel the icy coldness of the water until he was aboard the boat. Moreover, he recalled no stress during his swim beyond the time he was under water and gained his "second wind." When he surfaced, he felt "full of vigor." He credited his ability to undergo the ordeal to his physical, mental, and religious training. In all, 30 men, mostly crew members, ended up on the bottom-up boat. When it was fully occupied, those on board had to push away others who were trying to mount it. It was during this time that Gracie heard what he called a "transcendent piece of heroism that will remain fixed in my memory as the most sublime and coolest exhibition of courage and cheerful resignation to fate and fearlessness of death." This was when one swimmer was refused assistance and turned away. In a "deep manly voice of a powerful man," which Gracie did not recognize, Gracie heard the reply: "All right, boys; good luck and God bless you." The man then swam away.

One can only wonder if that swimmer might have been Robert J. Bateman, a 51-year-old Baptist minister from Jacksonville, Florida. A second-class passenger, Bateman had been visiting relatives in Bristol, England. He was returning to Jacksonville with his sister-in-law, Ada Balls. She later recalled: "Brother forced me into the last boat, saying he would follow me later. I believe I was the last person to leave the ship. Brother threw his overcoat over my shoulders as the boat was being lowered away and as we neared the water, he took his black necktie and threw it to me with the words, 'Goodbye, God bless you!'" Bateman's body was recovered three weeks later by a cable-laying vessel.

It is difficult to reconcile Ada Balls' comment about being the last person to leave the ship with the story of Edith Evans, who just missed getting on the last lifeboat after allowing her friend to board before her, but such was the confusion on that chaotic night.

During the time they waited to be rescued, several of the men on the overturned raft, unable to stand the cold, gave up the struggle and fell off. Gracie also recalled that he had been uttering silent prayers for deliverance when one of the crewmen suggested that they should all say the Lord's Prayer together. The suggestion "met with instant approval, and our voices with one accord burst forth in repeating that great appeal to the Creator and Preserve of all mankind, and the only prayer that everyone one of us knew and could unite in, thereby manifesting that we were all sons of God and brothers to each other whatever our sphere in life or creed might be."

TWO

PREMONITIONS OF DISASTER & DEATH

We can definitely affirm the reality of premonitions, not because all ancient writers, whether credulous or not, believed in it, but because many testimonies to it have been obtained in our own day.
— **Charles Richet,** M.D., Ph.D
1913 Nobel Prize Winner

In one of his many stories, *From the Old World to the New*, a novel published in 1892, William T. Stead described the sinking of a ship as a result of hitting an iceberg in the North Atlantic. The story involved an actual ship named the *Majestic*, captained by Edward J. Smith, who later captained the *Titanic*. One of the passengers on the *Majestic* was a psychic who saw the collision of another ship with the iceberg, thereby helping the *Majestic* to avoid such a collision and to pick up some stranded survivors from the sunken ship. Although the *Majestic* was owned by the White Star Line, having made its maiden voyage on April 2, 1890, two years before Stead's article, Captain Smith did not take command of the ship until 1895, some three years after the article appeared. The *Majestic* was retired in 1911, but then brought back to service after the sinking of the *Titanic* in order to fill the void in the transatlantic schedule.

In an 1886 story for *The Pall Mall Gazette*, titled *How a Mail Steamer went down in the mid-Atlantic*, Stead wrote about the sinking of an ocean liner and how lives were lost because there were too few lifeboats. Whether this story and that of the *Majestic* were some kind of precognition or "crystal vision" on Stead's part or merely coincidence is not known, but Stead apparently did not foresee his death as a result of the *Titanic* disaster when he booked passage on it. In fact, Stead claimed to have had a vision in which he saw himself being kicked to death in the street by a mob.

Nevertheless, Edith Harper, his secretary, reported that before his departure, on April 2, she lunched with him and sensed "an eerie sense of something too indefinable to call 'presentiment'" sweeping across her mind, something she had not sensed on his earlier trips. Stead went off to his cottage, Holly Bush, to spend Easter before departing for America. On April 6, he ended a brief letter to Harper, saying, "I feel as if something was going to happen, somewhere, or somehow. And that it will be for good..."

In a 1909 book, *How I Know That The Dead Return*, Stead, in explaining why he believes in life after death, wrote: "In order to form a definite idea of the problem which we are about to attack, let us imagine the grave as if it were the Atlantic Ocean..." He went on to draw a parallel between death's transition and the voyage of Christopher Columbus, suggesting that if Columbus had not been able to return within a reasonable time, Europe would have concluded that he perished and had not succeeded in finding a new land. While Columbus and his crew might have been thriving on the American continent, Europe would have regarded America as "that undiscovered bourne from whence no traveler returns," and their friends and relatives would have mourned the brave "who went out but who return not."

In a speech delivered by Stead to members of the Cosmos Club during 1909, he talked about what he felt to be overly strict barriers imposed by the Society for Psychical Research (SPR) in accepting communication from spirits of the dead. He pictured himself as shipwrecked and drowning in the sea, calling frantically for help. "Suppose that instead of throwing me a rope the rescuers should shout back, 'Who are you? What is your name? 'I am Stead! W. T. Stead! I am drowning here in the sea! Throw me the rope. Be quick!' But instead of throwing me the rope they continue to shout back, "How do we know that you are Stead? Where were you born? Tell us the name of your grandmother! Well, that is pretty typical of the 'help' given by the SPR to the friends who are trying to make us hear them from the Other Side!"

While the *Titanic* was being built, the Rev. Venerable Archdeacon Colley printed a pamphlet entitled *The Fore-Ordained Wreck of the Titanic* and sent a copy to Stead, who replied: "Dear Sir, Thank you very much for your kind letter, which reaches me just as I am starting for

America. I sincerely hope that none of the misfortunes which you seem to think may happen, will happen; but I will keep your letter and will write to you when I come back. Yours truly, W. T. Stead."

Just as mysterious as Stead's stories is an 1898 book authored by American novelist Morgan Robertson, initially titled *Futility*. The story involves a British passenger liner named the *Titan*, which was said to be unsinkable and carried too few lifeboats. During a voyage in the month of April, the *Titan* collides with an iceberg in the north Atlantic and sinks. In addition to the name of the ship, its nationality, its lack of lifeboats, and the month of the voyage, there are many other similarities with the *Titanic*. The *Titan* was proceeding at 25 knots, while the *Titanic* was going at an estimated 22-23 knots. The *Titan* was 800 feet long and had a passenger capacity of 3,000. The *Titanic* was 882.5 feet long and also had a capacity of 3,000 passengers. Some abridged passages from *Futility*:

> She was the largest craft afloat and the greatest of the works of men. In her construction and maintenance were involved every science, profession, and trade known to civilization... Unsinkable – indestructible, she carried as few boats as would satisfy the laws. These, twenty-four in number, were securely covered and lashed down to their chocks on the upper deck, and if launched would hold five-hundred people. She carried no useless, cumbersome life rafts, but – because the law required it – each of the three thousand berths in the passengers', officers', and crew's quarters contained a cork jacket...In view of the absolute superiority to other craft, a rule of navigation thoroughly believed in by some captains, but not yet openly followed, was announced by the steamship company to apply to the *Titan*. She would steam at full speed in fog, storm, and sunshine, and on the Northern Lane Route, winter and summer...at full speed she could be more easily steered out of danger, and...in case of an end-on collision with an iceberg – the only thing afloat that she could not conquer – her bows would be crushed in but a few feet further at full than at half speed, and at the most three compartments would be flooded – which would not matter with six more to spare...
>
> "Ice,' yelled the lookout. "Ice ahead. Iceberg. Right under the bows." The first officer ran amid-ships and the captain, who had remained there, sprang to the engine-room telegraph...in

five seconds the bow of the *Titan* began to lift, and ahead, and on either hand, could be seen, through the fog, a field of ice, which arose in an incline to a hundred feet high in her track. The music in the theater ceased, and among the babel of shouts and cries, and the deafening noise of steel, scraping, and crashing over ice...

Had the impact been received by a perpendicular wall the elastic resistance of bending plates and frames would have overcome the momentum with no more damage to the passengers than a severe shaking up, and to the ship than the crushing in of her bows and the killing, to a man, of the watch below. She would have backed off, and slightly down by the head, finished the voyage at reduced speed to rebuild on insurance money, and benefit, largely in the end, by the consequent advertising of her indestructibility. But a low beach, possibly formed by the recent overturning of the berg, received the *Titan*, and with her keel cutting the ice like the steel runner of an iceboat, and her great weight resting on the starboard bilge, she rose out of the sea, higher and higher – until the propellers in the stern were half exposed – then meeting an easy, spiral rise in the ice under her port bow, she heeled, overbalanced, and crashed down on her side to starboard.

The similarities between the *Titan* and *Titanic* pretty much end with the collision, although it is believed that the *Titanic*, in addition to the impact being on a side of the ship, did strike a submerged portion of the iceberg with the bottom of the ship.

Before both Stead and Robertson wrote their stories, Celia Laighton Thaxter, a popular American poet who died 18 years before the *Titanic* went down, penned a poem called *A Tryst*, which described a ship going to its doom after hitting an iceberg in the "desolation of the North" while traveling at "utmost speed." There were no survivors in Thaxter's poem.

Were these stories by Stead, Robertson, and Thaxter mere coincidence or did they have some kind of Nostradamus-like ability to perceive the future in what was some form of subconscious "crystal vision" which they themselves did not understand? In Stead's case, it seems clear that he did not foresee his death on a conscious level, but that he grasped it at the subconscious, or soul, level.

It is said that not long after the *Titanic* sinking, nearly everyone knew someone or that "someone" knew someone else who had booked passage or had considered booking passage on the *Titanic*, but for some unexplainable reason decided against it. They were saved by fate, by destiny, by their guardian angels, or by just plain luck. And so it is with many disasters. What ocean liner hasn't had someone book passage and then cancel for one reason or another. If the person cancels because of a death in the family or because of a business conflict and the ship later meets with disaster, the person is left to wonder if someone was watching over him or her. Who is to say?

John Coffey, a 23-year-old stoker on the *Titanic*, reportedly jumped ship at Queenstown after starting out at Southampton. When later asked why, he said that he "held a foreboding" about the voyage. However, since he lived in Queenstown, it may very well have been that he had never intended to go beyond Queenstown and the premonition was just a convenient excuse for not fulfilling his obligation to be with the ship on its full voyage.

Coffey may have been one of three observed by Elizabeth Dowdell, a third-class passenger, jumping ship in Queenstown. "I have crossed the ocean several times and traveled quite some, but in all my experience I have never met such a combination of superstitious people as were found among the passengers of the *Titanic*," Dowdell is quoted in an April 20, 1912 issue of the *Hudson Dispatch*. "We thought it but a joke at the time when arriving at Queenstown to have heard three sailors remark, they would not continue their contemplated voyage on board the *Titanic*, for they had a dreadful fear of some disaster. They got off at this stop and bade us farewell. But how true it was, after all. Oh, there are so many stories to relate that to me it seems as though I were in a dream."

According to a report in the *Washington Herald* on April 18, 1912, Jacques Futrelle, an American novelist, had a premonition of tragedy two weeks before he and his wife, May, sailed. "Turn down a glass for me," Futrelle wrote from Europe to a friend in Atlanta. He also sent his brother-in-law, John Peele, a power of attorney for the administration of their estate and provided him with a list of his bank accounts as well as directions relative to the care of their children.

May Futrelle survived in one of the life boats, but her Jacques perished. She detailed her experiences in her journal on the one-year anniversary of the tragedy. It is not entirely clear from her writing whether the dreams she mentions were in advance of the sinking or after it, but they seem to have been foreboding dreams in which she had nightmares about Jacques, seeing his body struck at sea by a ghostly ship. "I could see a look of terror upon his face in detail that was quite unreal as no such clarity would be possible from such a distance, his body being hurled a hundred feet or more by the force of the bow wave of the ship," she journaled. "And how could I witness this and still be standing on dry land when the body came back down? But such unreal things happen in dreams amidst a pervasive atmopshere of dread."

Anna Ward, the personal maid and companion to Charlotte Cardeza, reportedly told her mother that she did not want to take another voyage across the ocean. "She feared that something was going to happen, although she could not tell what made her fear another voyage," Mrs. J. W. Craig, her step-mother told the *Evening Bulletin* the day after the sinking. "We laughed at her and told her that her fear was groundless and she was persuaded to accompany Mrs. Cardeza. She said that it would be her last trip and it came pretty near being so." Both Ward and Cardeza were among the survivors.

Emma Bucknell, the wife of the founder of Bucknell University, is said to have told fellow passengers, Mrs. J. J. Brown and Dr. Arthur Brewe, on the tender at Cherbourgh, while waiting for the *Titanic,* that she feared boarding the ship because she had evil forebodings that something might happen. While boarding the lifeboat, Bucknell reminded Brown of her premonition.

An article appearing in the April 17 edition of the *Washington Herald* reported that Major Archibald Butt, an aid to President William Howard Taft, had, according to friends, several premonitions that "something terrible" was going to happen, although he was at a loss to explain it. He told his friends that he had never had such a feeling before. "His friends attributed these remarks to his unstrung nerves, and laughed them off. It was learned yesterday that Maj. Butt just before he sailed called three of his friends in and repeating these statements, asked them to witness his will."

The mother of John Hume, the ship's violinist, is said to have had a premonition that something would happen to him on the fatal voyage and pleaded with her son not to go. Hume laughed at his mother's warnings, and, along with the other seven orchestra members, was a victim of the disaster.

On April 17, 1912, two days after the *Titanic* went down, J. Cannon Middleton wrote the following to the Society for Psychical Research:

It may be of some interest to you to learn that on the 23rd of March I booked passage to New York on the White Star liner

'*Titanic*.' About ten days before she sailed I dreamt that I saw her floating on the sea, and her passengers and crew swimming around her. Although I am not given to dreaming at all, I was rather impressed with this dream, but I disclosed it to no one, as my friends, besides my wife and family, knew that I was about to sail on the '*Titanic*' and I did not want to cause them any possible uneasiness. The following night, however, I had the very same dream, and I must admit that then I was somewhat uncomfortable about it. Still I said nothing to anyone and had all my trunks packed, business affairs arranged, and in fact had completed all my plans to sail on the 10th instant. I therefore cancelled my ticket, and then – that is more than a week before the sailing of the '*Titanic*' – I told my wife and several friends of the vivid dreams I had had on two consecutive nights. I may mention that previous to canceling my passage, I felt most depressed and even despondent, but ascribed this feeling to the fact of my having to leave England – homesickness, in fact! I may add that crossing the Atlantic is nothing new to me, as I have crossed a dozen times during the past years, and I never remember having any feeling of uneasiness when about to do so, or during the passage.

Middleton further mentioned that a business conflict arose and that gave him a good reason to postpone his voyage. An investigator for the Society for Psychical Research contacted the two friends, both of whom confirmed that they were told of Middleton's dreams prior to the sailing of the *Titanic* on April 10.

Second-class passenger Lawrence Beesley, a teacher who survived, wrote a book soon after the sinking and dismissed the "superstitious beliefs" concerning the *Titanic*. "I suppose no ship ever left port with so much miserable nonsense showered on her," he wrote. "In the first place, there is no doubt many people refused to sail on her because it was her maiden voyage, and this apparently is a common superstition. Even the clerk of the White Star office where I purchased my ticket admitted it was a reason that prevented people from sailing. A number of people have written to the press to say they had thought of sailing on her, or had decided to sail on her, but because of 'omens' canceled the passage. Many referred to the sister ship, the *Olympic*, pointed to the 'ill luck' that they say dogged her – her collision with the *Hawke*, and a second mishap necessitating repairs and a wait in harbor, where passengers deserted her; they prophesied even great disaster for the

Titanic, saying they would not dream of traveling on the boat. Even some aboard were very nervous, in an undefined way. One lady said she had never wished to take this boat, but her friends had insisted and bought her ticket and she had not had a happy moment since."

Beesley's opinion aside, numerous veridical dreams have been documented with ship wrecks, seemingly a favorite subject of Stead's books and articles. He related the true story of a father of a son who had sailed on the *Strathmore*, an emigrant ship. In a dream, the father saw the ship foundering in the sea and saw his son and others on a deserted island near the wreck. The father told the owner of the ship of his dream, but the owner shrugged it off. However, when the ship was long overdue in port, the owner requested that other ships keep a look-out for any survivors on a deserted island along the intended route. After some time, the survivors were found.

Stead also wrote about the sailing ship *Persian Empire*, which left Adelaide for London in 1868. One of the crew, Cleary by name, dreamed before starting the voyage that on Christmas morning as the ship was rounding Cape Horn in a heavy gale, he would be ordered to secure a boat hanging in davits over the side. While carrying out his orders with another crew both were washed over the side and drowned. Although somewhat reluctant to join the ship, he overcame his fears and sailed. On Christmas Eve, as the ship approached Cape Horn, he had much the same dream. The following day, the scene he had seen in his dream began to unfold and when he was ordered to secure a boat hanging in the davits, he refused. He was taken below to face the captain and told of his dream. However, the captain apparently convinced him that he should carry out his duty. In so doing, he was washed overboard and drowned.

And yet another sea story related by Stead took place in 1853 and involved the Inman steamship *City of Glasgow*, supposedly the finest ship afloat of her class and kind. The ship's captain, Kenneth Morrison, was asked to depart Liverpool for Philadelphia, USA several days in advance of the scheduled departure date. One of the ship's crew, Angus MacMaster was on leave for 20 days and was unaware of the early departure date. As Morrison had taken a liking to MacMaster, who also served as Morrison's valet and entertained the crew with his violin, he asked his brother-in-law, the Rev. Alexander Stewart, who lived near where MacMaster was visiting, to summon MacMaster and advise him of the early departure. "To my astonishment," Stewart told Stead, "Angus replied, 'I am not going in the *City of Glasgow* – at least, not on this voyage – and I wish you could persuade Captain Morrison – the best and kindest master ever man had – not to go to either.'" When Stewart asked for an explanation, MacMaster replied in his Gaelic dialect, "Well, sir, you must not be angry with me if I tell you that on the last three nights my father, who has been dead nine years, as you know, has appeared to me and warned me not to go on this voyage, for that it will prove disastrous. Whether in dream or waking vision of the night, I cannot say, but I saw him, sir, as distinctly as I now see you, clothed exactly as I remember him in life; and he stood by my bedside, and with up-lifted hand and warning finger, and with a most solemn and earnest expression of countenance, he said, 'Angus, my beloved son, don't go on this voyage. It will not be a prosperous one.'"

Stewart informed the captain of MacMaster's decision and the ship sailed without him. The ship was never heard from again and it was the opinion of the maritime commission that it came into contact with an iceberg and went down with all aboard. Stewart added that Mac-Master was a Catholic and that Father Macdonald, his priest, told him (Stewart) that MacMaster communicated his dreams to him as well, precisely in the same terms as told to Stewart.

Warnings from the dead were also reported with Great Britain's giant airship R-101, which crashed in France on its maiden overseas voyage, on October 5, 1930. The R-101, a dirigible, was the largest airship ever built at that time. A little more than a year before its October 4th departure, warnings about the fate of the R-101 started coming through the mediumship of Eileen Garrett, a renowned Irish medium, from Captain Raymond Hinchliffe, who died when his plane was lost at sea during March 1928. (See following chapter for more on Hinchliffe.) "I do not want them to have the same fate that I had, as Johnston (the R-101 navigator) was a good friend of mine," Hinchliffe told his wife, Emilie, through Garrett. Emilie informed Captain John Morkham, her husband's good friend, of the messages. Morkham had come to believe that the messages from Hinchliffe were real as he had concluded that the technical language was beyond either Mrs. Garrett or Emilie. Morkham informed Johnston, but Johnston laughed it off.

"There will be an accident," Hinchliffe related at a later sitting. "I have seen Leslie Hamilton, and he agrees with me." Hamilton was a friend of Hinchliffe's who had been killed in a trans-Atlantic attempt during August 1927.

A similar warning from a "dead" pilot came to Stead to pass on to another pilot, Prince Serge de Bolotoff, who was to give a demonstration of his tri-plane at Chalons two days later. Stead was to cover the event as a journalist. While Stead and others were sitting with a clairvoyant, the clairvoyant said, 'I hear another voice speaking.' The voice then told Stead that "If you go to Chalons I will go with you."

Stead asked who was communicating. "I have been dead some time," came the response. My name is Lefevbre. Eugene Lefevbre was a stunt pilot who was killed on September 7, 1909, the first person to die while piloting a powered airplane. However, neither Stead nor the others sitting in the circle recognized his name at first. Another spirit began communicating and it was not until the next day that Lefevbre returned. By that time, Stead had figured out who this communicator might be. The dialogue recorded after that was:

Stead: "Ask Lefevbre if he was the man who was killed in the aeroplane accident."

Lefevbre: "Yes, I thought you knew it." (Stead had been abroad at the time and was unaware of Lefevbre's death.)

Stead: "You can communicate directly with me. Do you understand English?"

Lefevbre: "No, not much; but I transmit my thoughts to the medium and he translates them into English."

Stead: "What was it that caused your rapid fall?"

Lefevbre: "I did not have time to think. You scarcely have time to reflect when you fall."

Stead: "In your rapid fall did you keep your presence of mind?"

Lefevbre: "This is what I felt. I was conscious that I was falling, but before touching the ground I had lost consciousness. I felt no pain nor any sensation in my physical body. It seemed to me that my spirit was projected out of it. I had a sensation of rapid rotation, then something gave way suddenly, and I found myself in the air, seeing beneath my mortal remains and the machine. It was not disagreeable. I observed too that a being who was very powerful and who calmed me was near me."

Lefevbre asked Stead to warn Bolotoff that his motor would not work properly. Stead so warned Bolotoff. Bolotoff tested the motor and found nothing wrong with it and then took his seat in the aircraft. However, the motor would not then start and the starting handle broke. The demonstration flight was then abandoned.

One of the best documented stories of a precognitive dream is that of President Abraham Lincoln, who foresaw his own death by assassination about a month after the dream. But not all such stories are 100-200 years old. In her intriguing 2010 book, *Messages*, Bonnie McEneaney, the wife of one of the victims of the 9/11 terrorist attacks during 2001, tells of her husband having some kind of subconscious premonitions that his days were numbered. A week before the attack on the World Trade Center, Eamon McEneaney told Bonnie that he expected to die young and in the weeks preceding the attacks he seemed to have a sense that something monumental was imminent.

Monica Iken, the wife of Michael Patrick Iken, another 9/11 victim, told McEneaney that her husband began acting a little strangely during the summer of 2001. When they received an invitation for a December wedding, Michael told Monica that he couldn't see himself being there. Around September 1, Michael's behavior became even more abnormal. When, on September 10, Monica told Michael that she was planning to visit a sick family member in New York City the following day, Michael became upset and told her not to go to the city that day.

Bonnie McEneaney further tells of Welles Crowther, a 24-year-old equities trader who died in the attack. His friends and family noticed that he began acting very strangely during the summer of 2001. He was described by friends and family as being "depressed," and "restless," and, on Labor Day, his mother remembered that he seemed very "melancholy," which was not characteristic of him.

A woman named Lorraine told McEneaney that she had a dream a week or so before 9/11 that seemed to suggest that her husband, Bill, would meet with a tragedy. She didn't tell her husband about the dream, but she also observed that Bill's behavior and attitude the weekend before 9/11 were very different from what they normally were.

Sir William Barrett, a professor of physics at the Royal College in Dublin, Ireland, reported the case of a Captain MacGowan, who told him that, in 1877, he had promised to take his two sons to the theater in Brooklyn on a certain evening and had purchased advance tickets, but on the morning of the appointed day he heard an inner voice which repeated insistently, "Don't go to the theater; take your sons back to school." MacGowan attempted to distract himself, but the voice continued, repeating the same words over and over. He knew his sons would be disappointed if he were to cancel their theater plans. He explained to Barrett that the inner voice sounded "as if some one had really been speaking from the inside of the body," and that it persisted from breakfast-time up to the moment he took his children to New York. One hour before the play was to begin, MacGowan informed his sons that they would not attend. As it turned out, the theater was entirely destroyed by fire that night and 305 perished.

"I have never in my life had another presentiment, and I have not the habit of changing my mind without good reason, and on this occasion I did it with the greatest reluctance, quite in spite of myself," MacGowan told Barrett.

A Lisa Williams TV show of two or three years ago featured the parents of an 11-year-old boy who was killed in a boating accident off Waikiki in Hawaii. There was much evidential information passed on through Williams, a clairvoyant medium, to the parents, including the fact verified by his father that he did not want to go on the boat but was more or less forced into it by the parents. Williams told the parents that their son knew beforehand that he was going to die soon. When Williams mentioned this, the mother told her that after they returned home following their son's death, they found that their son left a message for them that he expected to be dying soon and looked forward to seeing his parents after they crossed over.

There are countless stories similar to those mentioned here, all suggesting that the soul, or the higher self, becomes aware of the fact that it will soon depart the earth plane.

In some cases, however, it is not person who is about to be affected who experiences it, but another person. It may come from an "inner voice," from a dream, or from a "spirit" of the dead. It might be called a "premonition," "presentiment," "precognition," "prevision," "second sight," "clairvoyance," "inner vision," "crystal vision," "extra-sensory perception" or some other name. These various terms take on different meanings with some psychical researchers and psychologists and may overlap or be completely synonymous in some cases. Clearly, they are not unique to the *Titanic*. There are indications that the more spiritually evolved the person, the greater the awareness. We don't hear about as many of them today as we did a hundred years ago, probably because modern writers and reporters are too skeptical, too cynical, too proud, too ignorant, or too fearful when it comes to reporting them, or people who experience them are reluctant for one of the same reasons to tell others of them.

It is unlikely that anyone collected more accounts of such premonitions and related stories than Camille Flammarion, a pioneering French astronomer, who documented many of them in a 1922 book, *Death and Its Mystery*. "In these accounts there is no imagination, nor illusion, nor trickery, Flammarion wrote. "They are as exact as a meterological or an astronomical observation. These studies have the rights of citizenship in science."

There were those who were unable to reconcile free will with seeing the future. "We can admit the premonitory sight of the future without compromising, for all that, the principle of free will and of human responsibility," Flammarion responded to them. "The present never stops: it is constantly continued by the future. Something will always happen; it is not inevitable for all that, if it is granted that the human will forms a part of the chain of events, and that this will enjoy a relative liberty; what it decides becomes real, but it might not have decided; the future is the succession of the past. This fact does not all prevent us from admitting that the human will is one of the causes of action in events. Something else might have happened than what did happen, and it is the other thing which would be seen in premonitions."

THREE

Apparitions &
Telepathic Messages

The examples of phantasms, of bilocation, of apparitions, are so numerous that it is impossible to rule them all out of existence and to deny their reality.

– Camille Flammarion,
Astronomer

On April 17, 1912, Mrs. Henrietta M. Chase, a resident of Groton, Massachusetts, wrote a letter to the Rev. P. H. Cressey, minister of the Unitarian Church in Groton, telling him of her strange visions at around 10 p.m. on Sunday, April 14. "I saw, being positively awake at the time, the face of a person," she wrote. "The face was entirely strange to me. It was that of an old man with hair and beard. The hair and beard were outlined in white, clear as light, and the features had a darker appearance. Marked lines between the eyes and an appearance of great suffering which had been smoothed away so as to give repose but somehow indicating an unbroken spirit were the features about this face that were most impressive. The face appeared to be below the level of my sight at arm's length. It was this that surprised me, this being the solitary instance in which a face appeared. I have seen many faces, flesh tinted, beautifully peaceful in expression, but they have all appeared erect and very very near my own face."

Chase went on to say that nothing ever came of the other faces she had seen, although she sensed a feeling of great peace after seeing them. However, this particular vision was very much different. On the evening of Monday, April 15, Chase read about the sinking of the *Titanic* in her evening newspaper. But somehow, Chase knew that some of the facts stated in the newspaper account were incorrect. "I knew intuitively that other news differing in character was to come," she further wrote, noting that her intuition proved to be correct.

On Tuesday, April 16, Chase told her daughter about the vision of a "face floating" before her, and at that time she sensed that her vision was somehow connected to the *Titanic*. "I hadn't a thought of 'them that go down to sea in ships,' and my only worries at that moment were of the weekly wash and the planning of breakfast and the hope that I could sleep well so to be ready for the day's work," she continued her report of her vision. "Indeed I recall all these thoughts as sordid, much so."

It was upon receiving the *Boston American* later that day that Chase was able to put a name to the face in her vision. It was William T. Stead, a British journalist who was on his way to New York City to lecture on peace at Carnegie Hall when he became a victim of the *Titanic*. Chase said that the face and beard in her vision were not quite as heavy and the face seemed younger in the photograph. "The other Boston papers followed with the same pictured face," she continued, "that of Mr. Stead, and in tonight's *Globe* the copy of Mr. Stead's photograph makes me willing to state positively that this is the face I *saw*, tho it does not, of course, reveal the trace of suffering which I plainly saw."

Chase also recalled a look of surprise on the face. "If asked to give my explanation of it, I should say that the mind of this individual acting with great force, like any other mechanism, had projected an image and I happened to catch it." She further noted a two-hour time difference between Groton and the longitude of the ship, putting her vision around 20-30 minutes after the collision. (Chapter One sheds some light on what Stead was doing at that time.)

Cressey reported Mrs. Chase's letter to Dr. James Hyslop of the American Society for Psychical Research. Hyslop questioned Mrs. Chase, who again stressed that she was wide awake and having a good laugh with her daughter shortly before seeing the face. While apparently accepting Mrs. Chase as a person of good character with no intent to deceive, Hyslop realized that the case was strictly anecdotal and of no scientific value "The case must rest with the narrative," Hyslop wrote in the January 1919 issue of the Journal of The American Society for Psychical Research. "It would have been much stronger if she had mentioned the fact before she saw the papers and if she had mentioned the name of Mr. Stead before she saw the pictures."

It is difficult to classify and evaluate this case, because Chase and Stead did not know each other. In most documented cases involving such a phenomenon, there is usually a connection of some kind between the parties, or it is not such a random connection. Moreover, if the time reported by Chase is correct, it was only 20-30 minutes after the collision with the iceberg and at that point few passengers really expected the vessel to sink The "know-nothings" and pseudoskeptics would no doubt dismiss Mrs. Chase's experience as a hallucination, or just a made-up story. However, the open-minded who are familiar with the volumes of research in the areas of traveling clairvoyance, out-of-body travel, bilocation, astral projection, telepathic communication, and remote viewing, all of which suggest that living humans have vision and hearing beyond their five senses, will likely see truth in her account.

"It is not only at the time of death that manifestations and apparitions occur," French astronomer Camille Flammarion observed. "It is often before." Among a number of other cases, Flammarion cited the case of Dr. C. J. Romanes, an eminent English scientist. Romanes reported that while he was awake in his bedroom, he saw a white form come into his room, grazing the head of his bed as it passed, and then come to a halt at the foot of the bed. "Suddenly, lifting its hand, the form withdrew the veils which hid its face, and I was able to distinguish the features of my sister, who had been ill for some time in that very house," Romanes reported. "I called to her, crying out her name, and I saw her vanish instantly."

Although his sister was ill at the time, her doctor did not consider it serious. Nevertheless, she died a few days later. "We may suppose that the subconscious mind of the invalid had a perception of imminent death, as opposed to the conscious personality which did not suspect it," Flammarion gave his theory. And so it may have been with Stead some two hours before the *Titanic* made its dive to the bottom of the ocean.

Still, we have to wonder why Stead chose the home of Mrs. Chase to project himself, if that is what happened. We get some clue as to a possible answer in the experiences of Hester Travers-Smith, a respected medium, as well as the wife of a prominent Dublin, Ireland physician and the daughter of Professor Edward Dowden, a distinguished Shakespearian scholar. Travers-Smith noted that she would occasionally get "drop-in" communicators – spirits unknown to her or those sitting with her. She would invariably ask them what drew them to her and almost always received the same answer. "They state that a bright light attracted them – and the stronger the medium, the brighter the light," she explained. "When I am sitting myself, and ask, 'What attracted you to this room?' the answer generally is, 'I saw a woman wrapped in flame.' Sometimes they describe a brilliant light on the head of the medium, but as psychic strength increases the light seems to envelop the whole body of the sensitive."

Some time on April 15, 1912, it is not clear exactly when, Mrs. Travers-Smith, still unaware of the fate of the *Titanic,* was sitting at her Ouija board with a friend when she received a very rapid messages stating: "Ship sinking; all hands lost. William East overboard. Women and children weeping and wailing – sorrow, sorrow, sorrow." Travers-Smith and her friend had no idea what the message meant and no more came through at that sitting. Later that day they heard that the *Titanic* had sunk. As a spirit claiming to be Stead communicated at a subsequent sitting, Travers Smith concluded that because of the rapidity of the message they got the last name wrong the first time.

Thus, Stead, in his out-of-body travel, may have been drawn by Chase's "light," and then later to Travers-Smith's "light," however such a "light" appears and attracts a spirit in another dimension of reality. Since there was very little in the way of land and habitation between Chase's home and the *Titanic,* her "light" may have been the first one he encountered, although it is not clear from the research in this area that land mass is a factor in such out-of-body travel. Of course, Stead may have encountered other "lights," which were not recognized as Stead or linked to the *Titanic.* We might also reason that the documented cases almost always involve loved ones or friends because the others have no meaning to the percipient and are therefore not reported.

On March 13, 1928, Captain Raymond Hinchliffe, a veteran pilot, and Elsie Mackay, a British actress and pilot, took off from Cranwell aerodrome in England in Hinchliffe's small plane, *Endeavor,* in an attempt to complete the first east-to-west transatlantic crossing. It was considered riskier than the west-to-east crossing of Charles Lindbergh a year earlier because of the head winds. They were not to be heard from again, at least in the flesh.

About 2 a.m. on March 14, Colonel G. L. P. Henderson and Squadron Leader Rivers Oldmeadow, Royal Air Force members who were acquainted with Hinchliffe but not close friends, were asleep on a ship in the Atlantic, headed from South Africa to England, completely unaware of Hinchliffe's flight. Oldmeadow was awakened when Henderson pounded on his cabin door. "Hinch has just been in my cabin. Eye patch and all," Henderson exclaimed. (Hinchliffe had lost an eye in the war). "It was ghastly. He kept repeating over and over again: 'Hendy – what am I going to do? What am I going to do? I've got this woman with me, and I'm lost. I'm lost!' Then he disappeared in front of my eyes! Just disappeared." Henderson needed three fingers of straight Scotch to calm down. It was not until three days later that they heard that Hinchliffe was missing and presumed dead. (Hinchliffe was mentioned in Chapter Two as communicating through a medium some two years later and warning of the R-101 disaster.)

As discussed in Chapter One, Colonel Archibald Gracie, who was still on the *Titanic* as it began its fatal plunge, was able to crawl onto an overturned life raft and survive. He later wrote of the ordeal and told of praying and saying to his wife, "Goodbye until we meet again in heaven." Mrs. Gracie later described what she experienced at the time. "I was in my room at my sister's house, where I was visiting in New York," she wrote in her husband's book, published in 1913. "After retiring, being unable to rest I questioned myself several times over, wondering what it was that prevented the customary long and peaceful slumber lately enjoyed. 'What is the matter?' I uttered. A voice in reply seemed to say, 'On your knees and pray.' Instantly, I literally obeyed with my prayer book in my hand, which by chance opened at the prayer, 'For those at Sea.' The thought then flashed through my mind, 'Archie is praying for me.' I continued wide awake until a little before five o'clock a.m., by the watch that lay beside me. About 7 a.m. I dozed a while and then got up to dress for breakfast. At 8 o'clock, my sister, Mrs. Dilliba Dutton, came softly to the door, newspaper in hand, to gently break the tragic news that the *Titanic* had sunk, and showed me the list of only twenty names saved...but my husband's name was not included."

Few such "visions" and "voices" are veridical, but so many of them have been experienced and reported to others that psychical researchers have concluded that they are not strictly hallucinations in the in the sense of being "unreal." They may be "unreal" to the five physical senses, but "real" to senses not recognized by mainstream science. In effect, a hallucination is not necessarily "unreal." They are unreal only in a materialistic sense. In his seminal book, *Human Personality and Its Survival of Bodily Death*, published in 1903, Frederic W. H. Myers wrote:

> There is one particular line of telepathic experiment and observation which seems to lead us by an almost continuous

pathway across the hitherto impassable gulf. Among telepathic experiments, to begin with, none is more remarkable than the occasional power of some agent to project himself phantasmally; to make himself manifest, as though in actual presence, to some percipient at a distance. The mechanism of such projection is entirely unknown to the agent himself; nor is the act always preceded by any effort of the supraliminal will. But our records of such cases do assuredly suggest a quite novel disengagement of some informing spirit from the restraint of the organism; a form of distant operation in which we cannot say whether the body in its apparent passivity cooperates or no.

What the Chase case and many others recorded by Myers and the Society for Psychical Research suggest is that we have a spirit body, etheric body, astral body, vehicle of vitality, double, doppelganger, mental body, whatever name be given to it, which is able to disengage from the physical body and travel great distances and make itself known to others in something of a ghost or phantom form. It is this spirit body that separates from the physical body at death. It is held to the physical body by an etheric cord, often referred to as the "silver cord." Once this cord is severed, death takes place, but some people, not physically dead, are able to travel, sometimes consciously, other times unconsciously, "out-of-body." The so-called near-death experience (NDE) frequently reported by researchers is an out-of-body experience (OBE) brought on by trauma of some kind, usually when the person is unconscious.

There are stories suggesting that the spirit body separates from the physical body before the actual physical death. Communicating through South African trance medium Nina Merrington, Mike Swain, who died in an auto accident, told his father Jasper Swain, a Pietermaritzburg, South Africa lawyer, that he left his body an instant before the cars actually impacted. Heather, his fiancée's young sister, was also killed in the accident. Mike told of being blinded by the glare of the sun reflecting off the windscreen of the oncoming car. "All of a sudden, the radiance changes from silver to gold. I am being lifted up in the air, out through the top of the car. I grab little Heather's hand. She too is being lifted up out of the car." When they were about 30 feet above the car, they witnessed the collision below them and Mike heard a noise like the snapping of steel banjo strings. They had suffered no pain. The "snapping of steel banjo strings" is a sound others have described in connection with the severing of the silver cord.

Although not then referred to as a near-death experience, Stead wrote of a "telepathic transmission" reported by Commander T. W. Aylesbury of Surrey, England. Aylesbury told Stead that at the age of 13 he fell overboard from a ship that was approaching the isle of Bali and was almost drowned. "After having sunk several times, when I came up to the surface of the water I called my mother, at which the boat's crew was very much amused; and they teased me many times about it, sparing no sarcasm," Aylesbury related. "Several months later, on my return to England, I told the whole story to my mother and said at once: 'While I was under the water I saw you all sitting in this room; you were working on something white. I saw you all – Mother, Emily, Eliza, and Ellen. His mother confirmed the statement and said she heard him call her, sending Emily to the window to look for him. Aylesbury figured the time difference and concluded that his mother's reaction was at the same time he was drowning.

Stead received a letter from Emily, Aylesbury's sister, confirming the incident. "We were seated and working peacefully, one evening, when first we heard a feeble cry of 'Mother!' We raised our eyes and said: 'Did you hear some one cry "Mother"?' The words had hardly left our lips when the voice called again, "Mother!" twice in succession. The last cry was stamped with terror, it was like a cry of agony. We all rose and my mother said, 'Go to the door and see what it is.' I ran into the street and searched for several minutes, but everything was silent and I saw no one; the evening was fine, without a breath of air. Mother was very much upset by this experience."

In his 1891 book, *Real Ghost Stories*, Stead further wrote:

Thrilling as are some of the stories of the apparitions of the living and the dead, they are less sensational than the suggestion recently made by hypnotists and psychical researchers of England and France, that each of us has a ghost inside him. They say that we are all haunted by a Spiritual Presence, of whose existence we are only fitfully and sometimes never conscious, but which nevertheless inhabits the innermost recesses of our personality. The theory of these researchers is that besides the body and the mind, meaning by the mind the Unconscious Personality, there is also within our material frame the soul or Unconscious Personality, the nature of which is shrouded in unfathomable mystery. The latest word of advanced science has thus landed us back in the apostolic assertion that man is composed of body, soul, and spirit; and there are some who see in the scientific doctrine of the Unconscious Personality, a welcome confirmation from an expected quarter, of the existence of the soul.

The strife to which recent researches into the nature and constitution of our mental processes calls attention concerns our conscious selves. It suggests almost inconceivable possibilities as to our own nature, and leaves us appalled on the brink of a new world of being, of which, until recently, most of us were unaware.

French psychical researcher and author Gabriel Delanne related the story of a curious apparition experienced by a Miss Paget of London. While in her kitchen one evening, she looked up and saw her brother walking toward her. "I cried out, 'Miles! Where did you come from?' He replied in his usual tone of voice, but very fast, 'For the love of God, don't say that I am here.' This happened in a few seconds, and as I sprang toward him he disappeared." About three months later, Miles returned to London from Australia and among his experiences he told his sister that while boarding his ship about midnight one evening he slipped and fell between the quay and the vessel. He recalled feeling that he was drowning and then losing consciousness before being rescued. In checking the date, Paget concluded that the vision of her brother was the same day he fell into the ocean, although the exact time could not be confirmed.

In *Phantasms of the Living*, pioneering researcher Edmund Gurney detailed the story told him by Robert H. Collyer, a physician. On January 3, 1856, Dr. Collyer's mother, Anne E. Collyer, living in Camden, New Jersey, was awake in her room when she saw another son, Joseph, standing at the door and looking at her. His head was bandaged and he was dressed in a dirty white garment, which appeared to be sleeping attire. "He was much disfigured about the eyes and the face," Anne Collyer set forth her recollection to Robert. "It made me quite uncomfortable the rest of the night." That morning she told her husband and four daughters of the vision. They wrote it off as a dream, and all nonsense. Then, on January 16, the family received news of Joseph's death as a result of a steamer, *Alice*, of which he was captain, being struck by another steamer on the Mississippi River, more than a thousand miles from them.

"My father, who was a scientific man, calculated the difference of the longitude between Camden, New Jersey and New Orleans, and found that the mental impression was at the exact time of my brother's death," Robert Collyer explained, adding that his brother, prior to his death, had retired for the night and was in his nightgown, his vessel moored alongside a levee when another ship collided with it. The investigation revealed that Joseph was called to the bridge as the other ship approached. Another brother, William, lived in the area and recovered the body, noting that Joseph's body was still in a badly soiled nightgown. "It will no doubt be said that my mother's imagination was in a morbid state, but this will not account for the fact of the apparition of my brother presenting himself at the exact moment of death," Robert continued. "My mother had never seen him attired as described, and the bandaging of the head did not take place until hours after the accident. My brother William told me that his head was nearly cut in two by the blow, and that his face was dreadfully disfigured, and the night dress much soiled."

Gurney received a statement from one of the daughters, verifying the facts as stated by Robert Collyer and adding that Joseph was killed when some part of the mast fell on him after the collision, splitting his head open. "My mother was not a superstitious person, nor did she believe in Spiritualism," A. E. Collyer, the daughter, testified. She was still awake at the time. It was not a dream. She remarked to me when I saw her in the morning, 'I shall hear bad news from Joseph,' and related to me what she had seen."

During May 1911, Stead wrote the Preface of a book titled *The Beginnings of Seership*, authored by his friend Vincent N. Turvey, who had taught himself how to leave his body and travel to places he had never seen. Turvey called it "mental-body traveling," referring to his mental body as his "I" and his physical body as his "Me," and explained it this way:

> In the mental-body traveling the 'I' appears to leave the 'Me,' and to fly through space at a velocity that renders the view of the country passed over very indistinct and blurred. The 'I' appears to be about two miles above the earth, and can only barely distinguish water from land, or forest from city; and only then, if the tracts perceived be fairly large in area. Small rivers or villages would not be distinguishable.

> When besides hearing – or seeing – with the mental body – 'I' also moves matter, then "I' makes use of a medium's psychic

force, which "I' appears to draw from the medium's wrists or knees as a sort of red sticky matter. At any rate, that is what appeared to happen when on one occasion "I" lifted a bed with two people in it, and spoke to them in the direct voice. Physically, I have not strength in myself to raise a small child.

In plain, long-distance clairvoyance I appear to see through a tunnel which is cut through all intervening physical objects, such as towns, forests and mountains. This tunnel seems to terminate just inside Mr. Brown's study, for instance; but I can *only* see what is actually *there,* and am not able to walk about the house, nor to use any other faculty but that of sight. In fact, it is almost like extended physical sight on a flat earth void of obstacles. This tunnel also applies to time as well as space.

As for the silver cord, Turvey mentioned that he sees the connecting cord whenever his "I' leaves his "Me." It joins the physical body to his "mental body," passing from the solar plexus of one to the back of the neck of the other. "It is very like a spider's cord," he further explained, "but in colour it is silver, tinged with heliotrope; and it extends itself and contracts in the same way as does elastic cord."

Dr. Karl E. Muller, who studied Turvey and others able to project their spirit bodies had no doubt that such experiences were real. "The whole field of exteriorization and astral projection covers a vast variety of observations which are not only of a subjective nature, but sometimes are connected with physical changes at the distant place," he explained. "The spirit body of projected persons has been observed by other persons, which proves the phenomenon to be real (in the usual meaning of the word) and not merely a subjective experience."

One such case was reported by the great German polymath Johann Wolfgang von Goethe. He reported that while he was walking with a friend one day, he was halted by an apparition of another friend, Frederick, who was believed to be in another city at the time. When Goethe started speaking to Frederick, the friend walking with Goethe thought he had gone mad, as he saw nothing. When Frederick vanished, Goethe wondered if his friend had died. Upon arriving home, Goethe discovered that Frederick was there, having a little earlier arrived in Weimar from his town, and then having gone to sleep in an arm chair while waiting for Goethe to arrive home. Frederic then related a dream he had had while sleeping in the arm chair.

He encountered Goethe and described the scene and words used by Goethe when Goethe saw him.

One of the people studied by Muller was Frederick C. Sculthorp, who developed the ability to leave his body after several months of experimentation. He explained that it required a state of extreme passivity in which he straddled the line between consciousness and sleep. At times, he seemed to be floating, then one night the floating sensation became a reality as he felt himself really rising, followed by a sense that he was vibrating violently. Initially, he simply wandered around his house while experimenting with his spirit body, but gradually became more daring and taking "excursions" to distant places. Sculthorp explained that the slight jerking or falling sensation people sometimes experience when about to fall asleep is the spirit body reuniting with the physical body, apparently when a sudden awakening signals a premature separation.

Stead wrote of seeing his friend, "Mrs. A." in church on October 13, 1895. He was surprised to see her as she was known to be very ill at home. Others in church also saw her and testified as to her presence. Stead noted that she seemed to be acting in an unusual manner. As she left early, Stead did not have the opportunity to talk to her at church, but he later visited her and found her still ill in bed, denying that she had attended church. Stead confirmed with her doctor that she was sleeping and under heavy medication at the time of the church service, thus concluding that he and the others had seen her "double" in church.

"This remarkable faculty which enables one to see details at such a distance, and in this case sense the personality without even moving from a position, is like telepathy, quite easy and natural in the spirit world," Sculthorp explained. "It seems that the spirit body is like an electrostatic condenser and charged with power. This power is at the disposal of the mind, and in the case of telescopic sight or telepathy, a fluidic feeler or surge seems to be projected naturally and automatically to wherever the thought is directed."

Flammarion mentioned many historical accounts of apparitions and related phenomena, including Cicero's story of "Uranie," a young man threatened with assassination who appeared to his distant friend and called him for help; the Baron de Sulza, chamberlain to the King of Sweden, who talked to his father at the entrance to their estate, while the father was in bed in the château; and the story of Bishop Alfonso da Liguori, who projected his image and thoughts from his convent in

Naples to Rome, to Pope Clement XIV, who was on his deathbed. "It would seem that we are concerned with a transmission of images by psychic waves between two brains harmoniously attuned, one serving as a wave-transmitter, the other as a receiver," Flammarion wrote. "Modern physics offers us examples that may point the way to the explanation, in telegraphy, photography, and wireless telephony. In this last case it is not words that travel from one point to another. They are broken up into Hertzian waves in order to pass from the starting point to their destination, where the detector recomposes them so that they may be heard."

Lest anyone think that such "expanded consciousness" is a phenomenon only of the past, the Monroe Institute in Faber, Virginia, USA exists today to facilitate the personal exploration of human consciousness. Founded by Robert Monroe in 1974, the Institute has had tens of thousands of students attend its residential and outreach programs. Central to much of the teaching is the out-of-body experience, a phenomenon which many of the students have mastered.

As Stead theorized, man had lost many faculties which he formerly possessed in the "attainment of self" through evolution. "It is at least conceivable that, as man loses old faculties, he may evolve new ones," he offered. "If he has lost the quick scent of the hound, and the balancing faculty of his simian ancestors, he may be capable of developing the faculty of far-seeing, or through-seeing, possible even that of foreseeing. By the agency of a wire and a cell he can hear the voice of his fellow across a thousand miles. Marconi has shown us that we can dispense with the wire. Who knows whether we may not some day dispense with the cell?"

Four

One Victim's Preparation for Death

Let us deprive death of is strangeness; let us frequent it; let us get used to it; let us have nothing more in mind than death. At every instant let us evoke it in our imagination under all its aspects.
— **Michel De Montaigne**

Even though William Thomas Stead did not have a conscious premonition of his death on the *Titanic*, he seems to have begun preparing for his transition at death well in advance of the actual event. That is not to suggest, however, that he was looking forward to his death or not enjoying life to the fullest. In fact, he apparently had a very full and active life right up to the time of his death, when he was on his way to New York City to give a speech on world peace at Carnegie Hall.

Stead's career as a journalist and author began during the 1860's when he became a reporter for a newspaper called the *Northern Echo*, advancing to editor in 1871. In 1880, he accepted a position as assistant editor of the *Pall Mall Gazette*, then became its editor in 1883. In 1890, he founded the *Review of Reviews*. He is credited with introducing the interview technique to British journalism and inventing the "New Journalism," bringing important topics in bright, colorful prose to the man in the street. Among those he interviewed were the Tsar of Russia, the Pope, British Prime Minister William Gladstone, Count Leo Tolstoy, and essayist Thomas Carlyle.

In a story written by B. O. Flower, the editor of *Arena*, a popular American publication, Stead is referred to as a cosmopolitan journalist "with a rare blending of intellectual force with moral conviction, idealism with utilitarianism, a virile imagination, and a common sense practicality that strove to make the vision a useful reality."

Certainly, Stead was not Kierkegaard's "Philistine" or anthropologist Ernest Becker's "automatic cultural man." Whereas those individuals repress the idea of death and immerse themselves in the mundane, preferring not to think about death, Stead had come to realize that in embracing death, what Socrates called "practicing death," one finds meaning in life and therefore better enjoys it.

The key to embracing or practicing death, as Stead understood it, is having a conviction that consciousness survives the death of the physical body. Such conviction, he believed, goes beyond the blind faith of orthodox religions and results from evidence, though not absolute, at least strongly suggesting survival. Stead found such evidence in mediumship. "Belief is one thing," he wrote. "Certitude is another. What we have to do is prove what is the fact so clearly that, as Mr. Minot Savage says, 'to doubt it would be an impeachment of man's intelligence.' It may be that we may fail in proving what we hope to be able to demonstrate. But the attempt may not be less fruitful on that account."

Stead believed that we are only "half alive" and that we can become fully alive by understanding more of the latent powers within ourselves and accepting the survival of consciousness. He wrote:

> The evidence and experiments of the [Society for Psychical Research] have already shattered, for one at least of our acutest scientific minds, all purely materialistic hypotheses. When dust returns to dust and ashes to ashes, the Ego lives on; the personal identity, the consciousness of the individual, does not seem to be momentarily impaired. It does not seem to be too bold a speculation to believe that the patient methods of inductive science, the careful examination of evidence, and the repeatedly renewed experiments of investigators, will before long completely re-establish the failing belief in the reality of the world beyond the grave, and leave us with as little room for doubt as to the existence of the spirit after death as we have now for doubting the existence of the Bering Straits, or of the Pyramids.

If Stead is still conscious of what goes on in the earthly realms, he must be surprised that his "before long" prediction failed, or at least did not succeed to the extent he may have thought. But he likely sees that it failed because of the opposition by both religious and scientific fundamentalists, those stuck in the muck and mire of their closed-mindedness.

"Personally I regard the fact of survival after death as scientifically proved," wrote James H. Hyslop, Ph.D., LL.D., professor of logic and ethical studies at Columbia University before becoming a psychologist and psychical researcher. "I agree that this opinion is not upheld in scientific quarters. But this is neither our fault nor the fault of the facts. Evolution was not believed until long after it was proved. The fault lay with those who were too ignorant or too stubborn to accept the facts. History shows that every intelligent man who has gone into this investigation, if he gave it adequate examination at all, has come out believing in spirits; this circumstance places the burden or proof on the shoulders of the skeptic."

Born at Embleton, Northumberland, England, Stead was first educated by his father, a Congregationalist minister, and later attended Silcoates School, Wakefield. The poems of James Russell Lowell played an important part in shaping his life's work, which, he decided, around age 18, was to help other people. While he remained a devout Christian to the end, he did not reject mediumship as so many Christians do. He did, however, approach the subject with much reservation. "It was with an uneasy sense of wrong-doing that I made my way to the haunt of the modern Witch of Endor, and sought from sorcery a vision of things to come," Stead wrote of his first séance in 1881. "I consoled myself by thinking that I could not waste my time more utterly by listening to the mutterings of the oracle than by enduring the dreary drone of Members, speaking against time, in an empty House; and silencing as best I could the uneasy suspicion of being a party to a vulgar fraud, I ventured into the nineteenth century substitute for the Cave of Delphi."

Like most people unfamiliar with genuine mediumship, Stead initially assumed that mediums are "fortune tellers," able to see into the future, rather than intermediaries between the living and the dead. Nor did he apparently realize that the "dead," at least the lower-level spirits who mostly communicate, are unable to see the future. As a result, he was not overly impressed with the first medium he observed. Although he often wrote about supernatural phenomena, he did not really become interested in mediumship until 1892, when he observed one of his office employees, the daughter of an Indian officer, do automatic writing. The woman was supposedly controlled by an entity known as 'Frederick,' whose handwriting was completely different from the woman's. On one occasion, Frederick told Stead that a "Mrs. D." was there and claimed that she could write through his hand if he were to give her a chance. Stead took up a pencil, his hand remaining absolutely motionless, but nothing happened. Using the woman's hand again, Frederick told Stead that he was not patient enough. He tried again, waited about five minutes, and gave up, telling Frederick that he was absolutely devoid of any mediumistic power.

A week or so later, Frederick wrote that Mrs. D. was there and begged for another trial. Frederick explained that he should try in the morning before he began work. He agreed to try it the next morning. "Before I had sat three minutes my hand began to move, very tremulously at first, and making marks that were at first almost intelligible," Stead explained the result. "After a little these marks became more legible, and, at last, slowly and apparently with infinite difficulty, a message was written out, imploring me to do what I could to save her son. When that one brief message was written the power seemed to be exhausted, and my hand would write no more."

On a subsequent attempt, an entity calling himself "Henry L." said he was trying to help Mrs. D., but he also failed to communicate a coherent message. Stead remained skeptical as to his ability to do automatic writing until some time later that year when, while staying at a country house, he gave it another try and messages began coming through from a woman named Julia Ames, an American journalist who had died the prior December, not long after a trip to London in which she interviewed Stead. Julia stated that the messages were for a mutual friend, referred to by Stead as "Ellen."

Stead wondered if his subconscious had been playing tricks on him and asked the invisible Julia if she could give him a test. Julia told him to ask Ellen what she last spoke to her about when she was alive. Stead's hand then wrote "MINERVA." Stead asked if that was a place and his hand wrote "No." He then asked if it is a person, perhaps Minerva the heathen goddess. Julia replied, "Yes." Stead replied that she wasn't making sense, but Julia said to just give the name to Ellen and she would understand.

Stead saw Ellen later that day and was told that she and Julia were discussing how the Woman's Christian Temperance Union had come into existence as a great power in America and that Julia had likened it to "the Minerva who sprang full grown from the temples of Jupiter" and had suggested that they call Miss Willard, the president of the organization, Minerva. Julia bought a Cameo brooch of Minerva and gave it to Miss Willard.

Figure 1 Abraham Lincoln, 16th U. S. president, foresaw his death by assassination

Figure 2 Spirits communicated in many languages through the direct-voice mediumship of Etta Wriedt, of Detroit, Michian, USA.

Figure 3 A retired British naval officer, Admiral W. Usborne Moore, studied mediums in Great Britain and the U.S. and was especially impressed with Etta Wriedt.

Figure 4 William T. Stead, a distinguished British journalist, was a victim of the *Titanic* but continued to communicate after his death.

Figure 5 The RMS. *Titanic,* the largest passenger ship in the world at the time, sunk on its maiden voyage. Considered a "floating palace," the ship. took 2 hours, 40 minutes to sink after hitting an iceberg.

Figure 6 Jacques Futrelle, an American journalist who perished in the Titanic disaster, apparently had a premonition of his death before the fatal voyage.

Figure 7 John Jacob Astor IV, thought to be the richest man in the world at the time, was one of 1,517 victims of the *Titanic* disaster.

Figure 8 Colonel Archie Gracie jumped from the ship as it plunged to the bottom and miraculously survived.

Although Stead was very much impressed with the test, he later asked Julia for another test. She told him that when Ellen and she were at Steaton, Illinois and going home together that she slipped on a curbstone fell down, hurting the small of her back. Ellen confirmed the facts as stated by Julia.

In a later message to Ellen through Stead's hand, Julia suggested that Ellen tell Lady Henry Somerset that she will not be able to keep her speaking engagement for the Temperance Alliance in Manchester because she will be in Denver. When Ellen informed Lady Somerset of the message, Lady Somerset said she had no plans to travel to Denver and saw no reason to cancel her speech. As it turned out, however, Miss Willard's mother died and Miss Willard was so grief stricken that Lady Somerset accompanied her to Denver for the funeral, canceling her speaking engagement.

Stead asked Julia how she could foresee things. "We can only foresee what is given to us to see," Julia replied through his hand. "We cannot see all that we want to see. For instance, I cannot foresee all that you are going to do. I can foresee some things that are going to happen to you, and some of those things I am allowed to tell you. There are other things I am not allowed to tell you. I am not likely to mistake what I actually see."

Curious as to how Julia could write with his hand, Stead requested an explanation. She told him that his mind was not "trammeled by the limitations of matter" and thus he was a good "instrument." She further told him that he could also receive messages from his friends still alive in the earth realm in much the same way. "All minds are in contact with each other throughout the whole universe," Julia explained, "and you can always speak and address any person's mind wherever that person may be, if you more or less know that person." She added that "your real self, what you would call your Ego, sits behind both your physical senses and your mind, using either as it pleases."

Stead decided to experiment by asking a lady in Gloucestershire to sit at 10:30 a.m. and try to make something known to him in London. They were to immediately post a letter to each other, she telling him what she was trying to communicate and he telling her what he received. Upon receiving the woman's letter, Stead was disappointed, noting that he had captured only one of seven distinct statements. But a few days later, he received another letter from the woman stating, "This is more wonderful than anything. You know that you have scarcely written anything that I willed you to write, but you have written nearly everything that kept bobbing into my mind without my will at all. When I was saying to myself, 'I want to tell you so and so,' it kept coming into my mind, 'tell him so and so,' and I thought 'No, that is of no interest to him,' or 'that will only trouble him,' and you have got all the things written down in London that kept coming as it were spontaneously into my mind at Gloucestershire at the time that I was willing to write another set of things."

The spirit "control" for another medium told Stead that he had a "very loose soul." When Stead asked what that meant, it was explained to him that his soul is very loosely connected to his body and thus he was "able to allow other minds to be hitched on" to his hand. Persons whose souls are closely knit, he was further informed, are not able to be used in that way.

Another communication from Julia involved one of his assistants, Ethel Morris. While Stead recognized her as a woman of remarkable talent, her "uncertain temper" was cause for him to consider terminating her employment. "Be very patient with Ethel Morris; she is coming over to our side before the end of the year," Julia communicated to Stead, who was startled by the message as there was nothing to suggest to him that Morris was likely to die. The message was repeated several times over the next few months and then in July of that year, Morris inadvertently swallowed a tack, which lodged in her appendix, resulting in her becoming seriously ill.

While Julia was communicating, Stead asked her if this was what she had foreseen and warned him about. "No," Julia responded, "she will get better of this, but all the same she will pass over before the year is out." As Julia had predicted, Morris recovered and returned to work. During December, she became ill with influenza and Stead again asked Julia if she would pass from this. Julia replied that this was not it and that she would not pass naturally. When the end of the year came and Morris was still alive, Stead told Julia that she was wrong. Julia admitted that she may have been off by a few days, but Morris' death was soon to take place. On January 12, Stead received a telegram informing him that Morris had thrown herself out of a four-story window in delirium and had been picked up dead.

As Morris was very interested in psychic matter, she and Stead had agreed to attempt to communicate with each other, whichever died first. Some weeks later, Miss Katharine Bates, one of Stead's many friends, was having lunch with a non-professional medium, Miss Rowan Vincent. "Do you know any William?" Vincent asked

Bates. "There seems to be some message from a William, as far as I can make out." Bates immediately thought of a cousin by that name who had passed over, but a few moments later Vincent, in a puzzled tone, said, "It is not *from* William – the message is *to* some William – I cannot understand it at all. Vincent then wrote down: "Dear William, I want to explain to you how I came to fall out that window – it was not my fault really – someone came up behind and pushed me out. Ethel." Having known of Ethel Morris' death, Bates asked for a surname or some other identification. Vincent then drew a circle and put a cross into it. When Bates reported this to Stead, he said that the cross within a circle was the sign that they had agreed upon to rule out an impostor spirit or fraud.

In her book, *Seen and Unseen*, Bates reported another very evidential sitting involving Stead. While visiting New York City in 1896, Bates sat with Mrs. Stoddard Gray, also an automatic writing medium. Julia communicated. Bates asked if it was Stead's Julia and requested her surname. "Julia O." was given and then another "O" added. Both Mrs. Gray and Bates assumed that the second "O" was a repetitive mistake. Bates asked where she had passed away, and Julia responded "America." Asked for a city, she responded with "Boston." She further communicated that she died in a hospital "five years ago" and that her age was 23. Although Bates knew of Julia, she thought that she was older than 23 and had died only "a few years ago."

That evening, Bates and several others sat with Mrs. Gray for physical mediumship. Julia materialized and took Bates' hand, but she was unable to speak or respond to Bates' questions. When Bates asked her if a mistake had been given in stating her age earlier in the day, Julia shook her head, "No." Bates asked why she couldn't speak, and Julia responded with "a little gesture of rather helpless dissent." Mrs. Gray then explained that spirits often use up all their strength in building up the materialized body and thus have no strength left by which to talk. Julia bowed her head in assent and then disappeared.

Upon returning to England, Bates passed on the information to Stead, not mentioning the second "O" in Julia's name. Stead then told Bates that Julia always signed her messages "Julia O. O." – a code name they had agreed upon, here again to rule out an impostor spirit or fraud. Stead also told her that Julia had already told him that she had appeared to Bates in New York, "but that she could not give you her name on that occasion, because she was not accustomed to speaking through the embodiment."

Skeptics claimed that such automatic writing, referred to by Stead as "letters," somehow came from the unconscious mind, even though such an explanation could not explain how the unconscious, or subconscious, mind communicated information unknown to the medium. "I am positive that the letters did not proceed from my conscious mind," Stead offered. "Of my unconscious mind I am, of course, unconscious. But I can hardly imagine that any part of my unconscious self would deliberately practice a hoax upon my conscious self about the most serious of all subjects, and keep it up year after year with the utmost apparent sincerity and consistency. The simple explanation that my friend who has passed over can use my hand as her own seems much more natural and probable. I have many friends, who, being still in their bodies, can write with my hand automatically at any distance. If this capacity be inherent in the soul of man, independent of the body, when incarnate in flesh, why should it perish when the bodily vesture is laid aside like a worn-out garment?"

Like other distinguished men and women who dared make public their beliefs in spirit communication, Stead suffered much ridicule. He wrote:

> No one who knows anything of the prejudice that exists on the subject will deny that I have no personal interest to serve in taking up the exceedingly unpopular and much ridiculed position of a believer in the reality of such communication. For years I have laboured under a serious disadvantage on this account both public and private. I am well aware that the contents of this preface will be employed in order to discount or discredit everything I may do or say for years to come. That is unfortunate, no doubt, but of course it cannot be weighed in the balance compared with the importance of testifying to what I believe to be the truth about these messages written in my hand.

In addition to the evidential material, Stead received many letters from Julia Ames describing afterlife conditions. He assembled many of them in a 1909 book called *Letters from Julia*. Some extracts from her letters follow:

> **On Dying:** I did not feel any pain in "dying." I felt only a great calm and peace. Then I awoke, and I was standing outside my old body in the room. There was no one there at first, just myself

and my old body. At first I wondered why I was so strangely well. Then I saw that I had passed over.

Soul after Death: When the soul leaves the body it remains exactly the same as when it was in the body; the soul, which is the only real self, and which uses the mind and the body as its instruments, no longer has use or the need of the body. But it retains the mind, knowledge, experience, the habits of thought, the inclinations; they remain exactly as they were. Only it often happens that the gradual decay of the fleshy envelope to some extent obscures and impairs the real self which is liberated by death.

Life Beyond: I find it so difficult to explain how we live, and how we spend our time. We never weary, and do not need to sleep as we did on earth; neither do we need to eat or drink; these things were necessary for the material body; here we do not need them. I think we can best teach you what we experience by asking you to remember those moments of exaltation when, in the light of the setting or rising sun, you look out, happy and contented, upon the landscape over which the sun's rays have shed their magical beauty. There is peace; there is life; there is beauty; above all, there is love. Beauty everywhere, joy and love. Love, love, is the secret of Heaven. God is love, and when you are lost in love you are found in God.

Many Realms: There are degrees in Heaven. And the lowest heaven is higher than the most wonderful vision of its bliss that you ever had. There is nothing to which you can compare our constantly loving state in this world except the supreme beatitude of the lover who is perfectly satisfied with and perfectly enraptured with the one whom he loves.

Judgment: It gave quite a new meaning to the warning, 'Judge not,' for the real self is built up even more by the use it makes of the mind than by the use it makes of the body. There are here men who seemed to be vile and filthy to their fellows, who are far, far, superior, even in purity and holiness, to men who in life kept an outward veneer of apparent goodness while the mind rioted in all wantonness. It is the mind that makes character. It is the mind that is far more active, more potent than the body, which is but a poor instrument at best. Hence the thoughts and intents of the heart, the imaginations of the mind, these are the things by which we are judged; for it is they which make up and create, as it were, the real character of the inner self, which becomes visible after the leaving of the body.

Outer Darkness: There is when the loveless soul comes here, as much care taken to welcome it as when the soul of love arrives. But the selfish soul is blind and dark, and shudders in the dark. The imagination, which here is far more powerful than with you, fills the solitude with specters, and the sinner feels he's encompassed by the constantly renewed visions of his deeds. Nor is this all; he sees those whom he has injured, and he fears. If ever a soul needs a Savior and Deliverer, it is when imagination and memory without love recreate all anew the selfish acts of a loveless life.

Higher Self: The Guardian Angel is indeed a kind of other self, a higher, purer, and more developed section of your own personality. This is perhaps a little difficult to understand, but it is true. There are, as well as good, evil angels, who are with us no less constantly, and they are also sometimes visible as Angels of Darkness when we come across. They are with us always, and we are with them here when we leave our bodies. We are always swaying hither and thither toward our good and evil guides. We call them, or we did call them, impulses, wayward longings, aspirations, coming we know not where or whence. We see on this side where they come from.

Divinity of Jesus: Oh, why do you trouble yourselves about these scholasticisms? The thing that matters to you is surely what is – not what may have been defined centuries since. My dearest friend, when you come to this side and have a more vivid sense of the majesty and marvel of the universe; when you see, as we do every day, the great unfolding of the infinite glory of the Infinite Father; and when you see also, as we do, that the whole secret of all things is Love, and that there was never so much Love revealed to mankind as in Him, you can understand how it is true that there dwelt in Him the fullness of the Godhead bodily.

Infallibility: We who have ceased to dwell in matter often make mistakes in our expectations, as you do, and err in our judgment. No one save Him who is above all knows all. We are not made infallible because we put off our bodies. We see many things you do not. But we are making progress through darkness into light, through ignorance into knowledge. And hence it is that while we may, and I hope often will, say what will help you and enable you to guide your way better, we never arrogate to ourselves the right to dictate. We are only too glad to impress you with our thought. But it is not Divine wisdom – only the thought of your friends who, being disencumbered of their earthly bodies, have the open vision, and dwell in the land of Love and Light.

Modern Revelation: Our chief difficulty in framing our message is the fact that we have nothing to say that has not been anticipated, more or less, by one or other of those messengers who have taught men the way to God. But this is obvious. You have to recognize the fact that God has not left you in darkness all these ages, nor has He given you misleading light. What we have to do is not to give you what I may call a revolutionary revelation, so much as to widen the chinks through which the same light may stream through a little more clearly. The fullness of the glory of that light we cannot describe. We who dwell in it are discovering more and more of the imperfection of our vision. And so it will never be. Progress, eternal progress, ever forgetting the things that are behind, ever reaching forward to those which are before it, is the universal law.

Reincarnation: Now life here being sensation communicated to the soul through its physical mechanism, what are we to think of life before and after? When I say *before*, you instantly think of reincarnation, about which I say nothing, but the pre-existence of the soul. All souls are eternal, being parts of the Divine Essence. For reasons known to Him who is over all, it is deemed essential that the soul should be passed through the training of physical life. It is part of the process by which the soul attains its ultimate evolution.

Passion to Know: For there is one Passion that increases rather than diminishes on this side, and that is the desire to know and to learn. We have so much to learn and such facilities! We shall never be able to say we know everything about this world, for the marvelous wisdom of God is past finding out. When we reach what we think the ultimate, there is a new vista of marvels which we see before us. We pass through, and when we come to stand, beyond us again stretches a new invisible marvel-world, into which we also may at some new stage of development begin to see. What oppresses us, if we may use the word, always and everywhere is the illimitableness of the universe. Up and down, we see it unfolding always and ever. When we make the most effort to exhaust the subject the more inexhaustible it appears.

Life's Purpose: Oh, my friend, if you would but see and understand what is the purpose of life, you would understand how fatal it would be to allow any and every cry for direction and guidance and help to be answered. And there are many who will, if the communications be opened, forget this and give advice and will attempt to direct those who consult them, and who will make sad trouble. For it is not for us to steer you. This object of life is to evoke, to develop the God within. And that is not to be evoked by allowing others to direct you. But you will find the purpose of the Father will not be allowed to be spoiled by the folly of His children, whether on this side or on that. Those spirits what attempt to interfere too much will be confounded. They will err, and be found out. Their authority will be destroyed. And so in the end things will come right again.

Society's Ills: For the whole of the evils that afflict society arise from the lack of seeing things from the standpoint of the Soul. If you lived for the Soul, cared for what made the Soul a more living reality, and less for the meat and drink and paraphernalia of the body, the whole world would be transfigured; you have got a wrong standpoint and everything is out of focus.

Julia's teachings provided Stead with a peace of mind that he did not previously have. He had moved from the blind faith of religion to conviction, and it was with such conviction that Stead courageously faced death on the *Titanic* that fateful day one hundred years ago.

FIVE

STEAD RETURNS FROM THE DEAD

I am personally convinced that the evidence we have published decidedly demonstrates (1) the existence of a spiritual world, (2) survival after death, and (3) of occasional communication from those who have passed over... It is however hardly possible to convey to others who have not had a similar experience an adequate idea of the strength and cumulative force of the evidence that has compelled [my] belief.

— **Sir William Barrett,** Physicist

William T. Stead is not listed among the 334 victims whose bodies were recovered as they floated in their lifejackets. Indications are that he was struck on the head, possibly by a falling ship's funnel, and sent to the bottom of the ocean. However, the evidence strongly suggests that he did "survive," though not in the flesh.

If the message received by Hester Travers Smith, as mentioned in Chapter Three, was not his first after-death communication, the first one may have been received by Dr. John S. King, a Toronto physician who had been exchanging letters with Stead and conducting telepathic experiments with him. That came through on April 16, 33 hours and 25 minutes after the disaster, as calculated by King, founder of the Canadian branch of the Society for Psychical Research. It was just a simple statement from Stead saying, in effect, that he would not be able to meet with King, as planned. As the message was apparently distorted somewhat in the filtering process through the medium's mind, it was not entirely clear at that point as to whether Stead understood that he had "died." The following day, April 17, a message came from Stead, saying, "I did not realize that death was the cause of my sudden harmony...I hope to be able to prove identity in several ways, not known to the hand that I use to write to you."

Meanwhile, back in England, on the second night after the loss of the *Titanic*, Lady Archibald Campbell, a clairaudient medium, heard the words: "W. T. Stead – drowned!" She was inspired to write and penned the following from the Stead "influence":

> There is at present nothing – no way to mark or show to survivors our varied experiences. To the rumour of waves, without recording apparatus, to the bottom of the sea went lost souls, for lost they were with despair coming in when hope was gone...Survivors there were who forgot the Divine law in saving themselves...I saw men and women lining the waters. It is difficult to picture to you how those people balanced there, half-paralysed, remained with thoughts asleep while yet unknowing of their re-birth. I do not come back to prose about what happened, which cannot be undone, but to give light to the strong, partly to implore those left on earth to subscribe prayers and messages of love to those who went under the waves. I am weary as with the pressure of all the ends of the earth upon me. But I will employ my vigilance as long as it is diplomatic for me to be upon this earth...I have much to do...

On his return trip to England, Stead was to have chaperoned Detroit medium Etta Wriedt to England so that she could again be observed and studied there. She was in New York City at the time the news came of the disaster, and according to her host, Stead came three days after his passing. "He was weak in articulation, but we quite understood him; his stay was short," Vice-Admiral W. Usborne Moore quoted the host. "The next night, Thursday, Mr. Stead came again; his articulation and personality were much stronger, and he went into details of his passing. The following night, Friday, he came again very strong and clear, again giving us full details of his passing. He particularly desired that Mrs. Wriedt go over to London to fulfill her engagement, which she is now about doing."

Moore, who had become a psychical researcher after retiring from the British navy, had studied Wriedt's mediumship on three different occasions and had suggested to Stead that she be invited to England. She had made her first trip to England in 1911.

On the night of April 18, Dr. King sat with Joseph Jonson, a materialization medium, in Toledo, Ohio, and both saw and spoke with King's deceased wife, May. King asked Hypatia, his spirit guide, who also communicated through Jonson, if Stead would be able to manifest there. "I cannot tell for certain," Hypatia replied. "I fear he has not power as yet to come and talk." However, as the sitting came to a close, Stead did appear. King recorded:

> As we neared the hour of closing, 10 o'clock p.m. – while all in the circle sat at ease, and were quietly talking – the curtains of the cabinet suddenly parted; and out there came, with arms extended, and with a determined, yet hopeful appearance, a man who walked straight over near to me, and was proclaimed by those who knew him, as William T. Stead. He did not speak, but retraced his steps until near the curtain of the cabinet, and melted – so to speak – from the view of all sitters.

As with all mediums, there were those who claimed that Jonson was a charlatan, cleverly tricking people with trap doors, confederates, and with whatever devices or means were employed by the real charlatans. However, King was very much aware of the fraud charges and means by which those posing as mediums tricked the public. When he first sat with Jonson during November 1911, he closely inspected the room, the materializing cabinet, the furniture and the single window in the second-floor room, taking every precaution to rule out fraud. There was a circle of six, including King, Jonson, Jonson's wife, and three others at that first Toledo sitting. After each of the other sitters had fully-materialized visitors come from the cabinet, May King, who had died 46 days earlier, emerged, caressed her husband, said a few words and then dematerialized in front of him. "As I stood there looking at her she got shorter and shorter in stature, and while still looking me in the face, she went down and down, in sight of all sitters, till she disappeared in the floor," King recorded. "Her voice in this, her first materialization, was not as strong as when speaking through the trumpet at Mrs. Wriedt's."

King's deceased brother, who had died at age 18 months, then materialized as an adult as did King's daughter who had died at birth 20 years earlier. Although King did not recognize either, he was able to ask them questions and confirm that they were who they said they were. The brother told King that he had been present along with many other relatives when May entered the spirit world. Still another materialized spirit for King was a man who had worked with King some years before and had died about three years earlier.

For his third 1911 sitting with Jonson, King had a stenographer accompany him to record the communication and happenings. There were 19 separate manifestations that night. May King was the eleventh to materialize. The stenographer recorded: "Beautiful and strong, and so convincingly natural as to overcome a strong man's self-control, Dr King's wife stood materially before him, speaking the following comforting words: 'Don't cry, dear Johnnie. My dear, this life is beautiful on our side....(some discussion about what to do with her jewelry)... Oh, Johnnie dear, I feel my strength going....'"

Back to 1912, on April 27, 12 days after the disaster, King again heard from Stead.

> Even my plight was preferable to some, for I was hurt by something like a blow, and so I quickly sank below the surface of the sea, no one will find my body, I can tell it now, for they (his afterlife guides) are aiding me to see it as a picture; and I know that I am one of the numerous ones who lie below the surface of the sea, and float away from touch of mortal hand. What better winding sheet than the great sea, so full of life and energy?

On April 28, Stead again communicated with King, mentioning that he "showed myself" in Toledo (through Joseph Jonson), which was a somewhat evidential statement. He added that he was initially too weak to effectively show himself and communicate and that his anxiety to do only hindered him. There was much repetition in the messages and the wording did not seem to be in Stead's style when he was alive, but King recognized that the medium's mind has to filter the messages and that it often colors or distorts them. Based on the force of the messages and some of the facts related, King concluded that it was indeed Stead communicating and not some impostor low-level spirit.

Back in England, Professor James Coates recorded that Stead manifested through his wife, Jessie, a trance medium, on April 26, in Glenbeg House, Rothesay. He said that Stead interrupted near the end of the séance and communicated:

> I am Stead. I know where I am. I was here before, but could not manage to make my appeal to all God-fearing men and women

for help. I wish to break in as my message is urgent. I am afraid I shall not make myself sufficiently clear. Knowing those here and the work quietly carried on, I thought it easier to break in here than elsewhere.

Could you but see the misery of those lost, as I saw them, your hearts would bleed for them. Called to part from all their cherished hopes, and from the new life which many of them looked forward to commence, to plunge into the terrors of the unknown – you would weep with and pray for them. May you all take the lesson out of this sad catastrophe, that God intends you to take.

Vaunt not in your riches and possessions on earth, the homage of men or the praise of kings, for all these things are as dross compared with the consciousness of the nearness of God: his infinite love and assurance of life immortal. Did you ponder on these things, your eyes would be opened to take the path you are intended to take. With clearer vision, you would seek the Master, Christ, our Lord, and learn of Him.

Many of those who passed into eternity with me do not know where they are. It was a stunning blow and a terrific reversal of all their ideas and plans. Few there were who entertained thoughts of this life. Many were full of hopes of what was in store for them in the immediate future on earth; life was bright to many of them. Others were faithfully discharging duties when the call came with tragic swiftness. I was surprised, appalled, and yet assured. When the end came, it was merciful, painless....

Many who went under became quickly conscious of the change and are working to help others who are lost in confusion and darkness. It is terrible to witness the sad state of these. Pray for them. Send my message out to all who knew me, to pray for those poor souls. Rich or poor on earth, what does it matter; they have been cut off from all they looked upon as life. Pray that they may be liberated and illuminated. Pray that they may see the light...

I saw ministering spirits, glorified spirits, helping the feeble ones whose bodies went down with the vessel or perished in the numbing waters. They were arousing those, brave or terror-stricken, who had faced the reality. Many soon realized the great change had come, but the majority are as blind as bats. They cannot help themselves. Pray for them...

Stead's communication through Jessie Coates was widely circulated in newspapers in the United Kingdom, United States, India, and Australia, although it was ridiculed by some. While there was nothing particularly evidential in the statement, the Rev. Dr. Charles Hall Cook, who was present, called the message in "the ethics and style of Stead."

On May 3, Stead again communicated through Mrs. Coates, mentioning that he could not describe the afterlife environment. "I could not conceive, even faintly, on earth, what the joys of this life would be," his words were recorded. "The freedom is beyond expression; it is new life indeed. Such glimpses of my surroundings as I have been able to obtain are glorious beyond expression. Rejoice with me, although I cannot convey to you the fullness of my joy."

Madam Lily Laessoe, an automatic writing medium living in Copenhagen, Denmark, claimed to have taken dictation from Stead on May 23. He told of what would today be called a "near-death experience," in which deceased loved ones were with him. "I think that my head was struck by something, and that I lost consciousness outwardly; but *inwardly* I was wide awake, and it was those last moments I spent with my loved ones."

Upon arriving in England, Etta Wriedt gave her first sitting on May 5, 1912, 20 days after Stead's death. "This American woman has a mysterious gift which enables those who sit in the same room with her to learn of the continued existence of those whose physical bodies have perished," Admiral Moore explained. "The possession of this strange power is acquired by no virtue of her own; she was born with it. Unlike the gifts of poetry, art, oratory, or song, it demands from her no effort; and with proper precautions, it causes no strain upon her physical constitution." Wriedt was observed by Moore and others talking to people sitting next to her at the same time as spirit voices came through. It was reported that as many as four spirit voices would be talking simultaneously to different sitters and, although Wriedt knew only English, spirits communicated in French, German, Italian, Spanish, Norwegian, Dutch, Arabic and other languages. While voices could be heard in lighted conditions, they were stronger in the dark.

According to Moore, Stead first manifested on May 6 at Cambridge House, Wimbledon, Stead's country residence, giving "three admirable tests of his identity," including some details about a conversation Stead and Moore had had at a bank building the last time they met. Estelle Stead, Stead's daughter wrote her account:

I went down to Cambridge House full of grief, sorrow, and bewilderment, wondering and hoping. I was not alone at the sitting; several others were present. The scent of flowers filled the room, and there was a feeling of awe and expectancy in the air. The lights were turned off, and for a few moments we sat in darkness; then came a bright light, followed by the etherealisation of one I admire and love, who passed over into spirit life some years ago; this passed, and in its place I saw my father's face. For a few seconds I gazed, hardly able to realize that he had indeed passed over and was not physically among us in the circle as of old. Then the etherealisation faded, and in a few seconds his voice rang through the room. He spoke to me, and for a little time our emotion overcame us, and then he bade me not to grieve. But he himself was full of grief at having to go when there was still much to be done – 'if only he could come back for an hour' – and I found myself comforting him. It was a meeting full of anguish, mingled with joy. He talked of home matters, of people, of arrangements, etc., all unknown to Mrs. Wriedt or the other sitters.

Estelle Stead said that she talked with her father for over twenty minutes, but Moore estimated that it was closer to 40 minutes and described it as the most painful but most realistic and convincing conversation he had heard during his investigations of mediumship. He said that Stead gave detailed instructions to his daughter as to the disposal of his private papers.

Two days later, at least 15 different spirits communicated with the sitters. Stead came about the middle, Moore wrote, talking loudly. "Ladies and gentlemen, I beg to propose that these sittings be continued, at any rate as long as Mrs. Wriedt is here," Moore quoted Stead. "Those in favour, hold up their hands. If any money is required I will see to it. (pause) Admiral Moore, you have not held up your hand." Moore noted that it was pitch dark, but to humour Stead he then raised his hand, after which his head was struck twice by the trumpet.

It was on May 8, Moore recorded, that Captain Smith of the *Titanic*, made himself known through Wriedt's mediumship and assumed full blame for the disaster. On May 15, a physician interested in psychical research attended and was greeted by Stead. Two other spirits communicated with the doctor, one being a patient who had died the previous year, asking the doctor if he had ever been paid for his services. This was very evidential to the doctor as there was some delay by the executors of the estate in paying his bill. Another sitter, Ella Anker, was visited by her deceased daughter, who spoke Norwegian to her mother. Moore noted that two voices, occasionally three, would at times be talking simultaneously to the various sitters.

Count Chedo Miyatovich, a diplomat from Serbia, sat with Mrs. Wriedt on May 16, 1912, accompanied by his friend, Dr. H. Hinkovitch. Miyatovich documented his observation:

> I and Dr. Hinkovitch took seats near each other in the centre of the room, facing the cabinet. Mrs. Wriedt did not enter the cabinet, but sat all the time on a chair near me. She placed a tin speaking tube (megalophon) in front of my friend. She started an automatic musical clock and put all the lights out, so that we sat in perfect darkness. When a beautiful melody of a somewhat sacred character was finished by the clock, Mrs. Wriedt said to us that the conditions were very good, and that we should be able not only to hear, but also to see some spirits. 'Yes,' she continued, 'here is the spirit of a young woman. She nods to you, Mr. Miyatovich; do you not see her?' I did not, but my friend saw an oblong piece of illuminated mist. Mrs. Wriedt then said that the woman whispered to her that her name was Adela or Ada Mayell. I was astounded. Only three weeks before died Miss Ada Mayell, a very dear friend of mine, to whom I was deeply attached. The next moment a light appeared behind Mrs. Wriedt and moved from left to right. There in that slowly moving light was, not the spirit, but the very person of my friend William T. Stead, not wrapped in white, but in his usual walking costume. Both I and Mrs. Wriedt exclaimed loudly for joy. Hinkovitch, who knew Stead only from photos, said: 'Yes, that is Mr. Stead.' Mr. Stead nodded to me and disappeared. Half-a-minute later he appeared again, looking at me and bowing; again he appeared, and was seen by all three of us more clearly than before. Then we all three distinctly heard these words: 'Yes, I am Stead. William T. Stead. My dear friend, Miyatovich, I came here expressly to give you fresh proof that there is life after death, and that Spiritism is true. I tried to persuade you of that while here, but always hesitated to accept the truth.' There I interrupted him by saying: 'But you know I always believed what you said to me!'

'Yes,' he continued, 'you believed because I was telling you something about it, but now I come here to bring you proof of what I was telling you – that you should not only believe, but know [pronouncing that word with great emphasis] that there is really a life after death, and that Spiritism is true! Now, good-bye my friend! Yes, here is Adela Mayell, who wishes to speak to you!'

Stead never knew Miss Ada Mayell in his life, nor had he ever heard her name before. She then spoke to me in her affectionate and generous manner, trying to reassure me on certain questions which have sadly preoccupied my mind since her death, and telling me that she is happy now. There is no need to report here all she said to me. Mrs. Wriedt and Mr. Hinkovitch heard every word she said.

Then, to my own and my Croatian friend's astonishment, a loud voice began to talk to him in the Croatian language. It was an old friend, a physician by profession, who died suddenly from heart disease. My friend Hinkovitch could not identify who that might have been, but they continued for some time the conversation in their native tongue, of which, naturally, I heard and understood every word. Mrs. Wriedt, for the first time in her life, heard how the Croatian language sounds…

I and my Croatian friend were deeply impressed by what we witnessed on that day, May 16, between 11 and 12 o'clock at noon. I spoke of it to many of my friends as the most wonderful experience of my life.

Miyatovich told his friend, Frau Professor Margarette Selenka of Germany, also a friend of Stead's, of his experience and they arranged a private sitting with Mrs. Wriedt on Friday, May 24 at 1 p.m. However, nothing happened. They returned at 8 p.m. and were joined by Edith Harper and her daughter. Miyatovich described what then took place:

After a short time from the beginning of the séance we all saw Mr. Stead appear, but hardly for more than ten seconds. He disappeared, to reappear again somewhat more distinctly, but not so clearly as he appeared to me on May 16. That was the only materialization phenomenon of that evening, but as compensation we had wonderful and various voicing manifestations. Mr.

Stead had a long conversation with Mme. Selenka and a short one with me, reminding me of an incident which, two years ago, took place in his office at Mowbray House. Then, again, Miss Ada Mayell spoke to me, telling me, among other things, that she knew that her sisters and her niece wrote to me, as she wished them to do. After her, my own mother came and spoke to me in our Servian language most affectionately. Mme. Selenka had a very affecting conversation with her husband, Professor Lorentz Selenka, of the Munich University, and also with her own mother, who died last year in Hamburg; both these conversations were carried on in German. A friend of Mme. Selenka came singing a German song, and asked her to join him, as they used to sing together in old times, and Mme Selenka did join him singing. Then we had an Irishman, once a naval officer, who had a long, cheerful and indeed, quite a sparkling talk with the charming lady, whose name I unfortunately do not know, but with whom the brilliant Irishman seemed to be everlastingly in love. Naturally, although I heard clearly all the conversations in German and English, I am not justified in reporting them here...All I wish to state publicly is that I am deeply grateful to the wonderful gift of Mrs. Wriedt for having enabled me to obtain from my unforgettable friend, William T. Stead, a convincing proof that there is a life after death, and that Spiritism is true, and for having given me almost a heavenly joy in hearing the affectionate words of my dear mother in our own tongue, and in getting another and sacred proof of the continuance of the living individuality of one of the most charming, most selfless, and generous women whom I have ever known so far in my life.

At a subsequent sitting, Moore heard from several relatives and two friends. "The chief communicator was Iola (a deceased relative), who told me many new truths and evinced the most extraordinary memory for events ranging over a period of form forty to fifty years," Moore wrote. "She recalled to me circumstances that occurred during my voyages about Australia, showing a familiarity with numerous events that did not take place till four years after her death."

Like Dr. John King, Moore had also sat with Joseph Jonson of Toledo and had become familiar with Grayfeather, Jonson's spirit guide. Moore reported that Grayfeather communicated a number of times through Mrs. Wriedt's mediumship in England. Moore observed that rain seemed to negatively affect the sitting with Mrs. Wriedt. Dr. Sharp spoke often, usually in a loud, clear voice. Moore further noted what he had experienced in his sittings with Mrs. Wriedt in Detroit, that the voices came through her in lighted conditions, but they were much stronger in the dark.

At one of the sitting, Moore recorded, a spirit communicated with Mrs. Wriedt, informing her that her husband, who was back in Detroit, had slipped on some steps and strained his ankle. This was later verified as true.

Another interesting account was given by Mr. J. Maybank, who, along with his wife, attended a May 20 sitting with Mrs. Wriedt. Maybank had once served on a ship commanded by Moore but was then employed as a civil servant. The Maybanks' 22-year-old son, Harold, had died from consumption on February 24, 1911. Although not directly involving Stead, Maybank's testimony clearly gives credibility to Mrs. Wriedt and the genuineness of the Stead manifestations. Maybank reported:

> We sat in a semi-circle, Mrs. Wriedt sitting at one end of the arc, and after taking our seats all light was excluded by heavy curtains over the windows, etc. The Lord's prayer was then repeated aloud, and then one verse of that beautiful hymn, 'Lead Kindly Light,' was sung by all present, and lovely voices from all parts of the room were heard joining in the singing. A voice then pronounced the benediction, individually, in Latin, and we were told it was Cardinal Newman who was speaking. The hymn, 'There are angels hovering around,' was next sung, and my wife and I were conscious of bright forms floating around the room. There forms were not recognized by us, but we undoubtedly saw them. I propose to omit all that happened which did not directly concern us, and only mention the facts we experienced and can vouch for. We were all sitting quietly and expectantly when Mrs. Wriedt exclaimed, "There is someone at the roses!" and a lady next to me said, "I have a rose," and another and another said the same. I then felt a splash of water on my forehead, and immediately after a rose with a long stem dropped into my hand, which I passed to my wife.
>
> Directly after this an uncle and a great uncle and great aunt of my wife came and spoke through one of the trumpets previously mentioned. The conversation that ensued was purely personal and private, and would not be of interest to the general reader,

but it left no doubt in my mind that I was actually conversing with those who had departed from this life many years ago...

Maybank then told of hearing from a spirit whose name had been Tommy Mahone when alive. Mahone was an old shipmate of Maybank's, also having served under Moore's command on a ship named *Rambler*. Initially, Maybank did not recall him, but when Mahone referred to several incidents that happened on the China station, Mahone remembered him. Although Moore did not recall Mahone, he apparently recalled the incidents.

Such stories as this, Moore observed, are clearly in conflict with the claim that all such "spirit" messages are simply the result of telepathy, or mindreading, on the part of the medium.

Harold Maybank then communicated, telling his parents that he was perfectly sound and with his mother's grandmother. Harold said that it was he who placed the rose in his father's hand to give to his mother.

The Maybanks returned the following night. Stead came and spoke to some in the circle for quite a long time, after which Harold again communicated. Although certain he was hearing from his son, Maybank decided to give him a test question – one that would be absolutely convincing. He asked Harold if he remembered poor old Cyril. "Of course I do, dad; didn't I tease him?" Harold responded through the trumpet. "And didn't he growl?" At that point, Harold growled through the trumpet, causing the sitters to laugh. Cyril was the family cat and Maybank was certain that no one in the room knew of Cyril.

In a third sitting by the Maybanks, Harold actually showed himself. "We both distinctly saw and recognised him," Mr. Maybank wrote. "He expressed his pleasure at seeing us, and thanked the Admiral for his kindness in affording us this opportunity to come into communication with him. Mrs. Maybank then heard from her sister, Flossie, who had died 27 years earlier at age three. Flossie said that she was a woman now and referred to the last time she saw her sister, when Mrs. Maybank was leaving on a trip to China, a very evidential and convincing point for Mrs. Maybank.

A witness who preferred to be identified only as "M.E." sat with Wriedt on May 25 and reported seeing Stead. "I now noticed ovals of light floating about the cabinet, but could not see any detail," M.E. reported. "But those who had better psychic vision than myself described them as men's faces. Suddenly there appeared a very bright oval light above the cabinet, and I distinctly saw the face of Mr. Stead, who seemed to bow to the company and then disappear. Almost immediately after, a strong voice asked: 'Did you see me?' One or two ladies replied: 'Yes, Mr. Stead.' The voice replied: 'I am not speaking to the ladies, but to the gentleman.' Then, addressing me by name, he said, 'How do you do?" I am pleased to see you here.' (I knew Mr. Stead when he lived in the North.) Voices continued to speak afterwards, but with no great success, and Mrs. Wriedt decided to close the séance, which was done by singing a closing hymn."

Moore related the experience of a Dutch lady, who sat with Wriedt on May 14, accompanied by her son and sister. During a few moments of silence, her young son began to whistle a tune, which was repeated by spirit. Stead then spoke in a very husky voice and said to the boy, "You are the young man who came to my office in a very depressed state of mind." The mother confirmed that her son had indeed met Stead under those very circumstances.

At a sitting on June 4, with Edith Harper and Lt. General A. Phelps present, Stead communicated and told Harper that other mediums around the world were getting his messages wrong and that he is not strong enough to effectively use anyone's magnetism. Stead greeted General Phelps, after which Phelps heard from his deceased wife. They spoke about their children and grandchildren before Phelps asked his wife how long it took her to recover consciousness after her passing. "Three days," she responded. Phelps then asked if she recovered her "clarity of sense" at the same time. His wife replied that it took nine to ten days for that. "Then your mind was clouded? Phelps asked. "No, no; it was just like a dream, as though you were in a slumber, dreaming and then I really pulled myself together – I found I had gone into another sphere," she replied.

Major-General Sir Alfred Turner, a retired British army officer, recorded his first experience in hearing from Stead, about April 25, 1912.

About ten days after the foundering of the monster ship I held a small and carefully selected séance in my house. No professional medium was present, but Mr. Stead's private secretary and her mother (who lived at Cambridge House, Wimbledon) were among the sitters. We had hardly commenced when a voice, which came apparently from my behind my right shoulder, exclaimed, 'I am so happy to be with you again!' The voice was unmistakably that of Stead, who immediately (though not visible to anyone) commenced to tell us of the events of the dire moments when the huge leviathan settled down to her doom, and slowly sank to her grave two miles below the surface of the sea. For himself, he felt no fear whatever. He had premonition of his physical ending, as we know, from the last letter written by him from Cherbourg a few days before the disaster, that he felt that the greatest event of his life was impending, but he knew not what it was. When the *Titanic* sank there was, as regards himself, a short, sharp struggle to gain his breath, and immediately afterwards he came to his senses in another state of existence. He was surrounded by hundreds of being, who, like himself, had passed over the bourne, but who were utterly dazed, and being, at all events for the part, totally ignorant of the next stage of life to come, were groping about as in the dark, asking for light, and entirely unconscious that they were not still in the flesh. He set himself at once to do missionary work by enlightening these poor and unprepared creatures; and in such work, he told, us, he was still employed, with the assistance of numerous spirit inhabitants of the next plane, whose task and bounden duty is to help and enlighten those who pass over. I can well imagine the contemptuous sneers of many who sit in the seats of the scornful on reading the above, and whose extend of belief is limited to their powers of comprehension – not an excessive quantity as a rule.

Stead had then a long conversation with his secretary, during which he gave some instructions to her. Asked by me if he would show himself to us, he replied: 'Not tonight, but if you go to Cambridge House on such and such a day, I will do so. The voice then died away.

General Turner went to Cambridge house on the day prescribed by Stead in his initial communication with him and found a large and incongruous circle with Mrs. Wriedt. "As he had promised, Stead appeared twice in rapid succession," Turner wrote. "He was dressed in his usual attire, so familiar to all his friends, and looked supremely happy. He remained only a few moments in each case, and said nothing. Mrs. Wriedt was the medium. We had no further manifestations of any kind, at which I was not surprised." Turner again visited Cambridge House to sit with Wriedt, once more finding an incongruous circle, which sat for over an hour with no results. Turner felt that the incongruity of the circle obstructed the spirits, mentioning that a harmonious state of mind of the sitters is necessary for results and that incredulity, especially scoffing, deters results.

On May 29, William Stead, Jr., who died in 1907, talked with his sister, who told Moore that the voice was exactly the same as she remembered it. Also, one of the sitters heard from Theodore Brailey, another victim of the *Titanic*.

On June 3, Estelle Stead and her living brother had a private sitting with Mrs. Wriedt. The lights were put out and the music box turned on. Estelle reported:

> Presently, we saw a light in the cabinet, and in a few minutes we saw father's face etherealized. He came right out of the cabinet over us. It was not quite so clear an etherealisation as the first time I saw him, but it was unmistakably father. He seemed to be holding his hand to his face. He disappeared and presently we saw him again; this time he did not move from the cabinet, and the etherealisation was clearer. He turned to my brother and to me and smiled. My brother said he saw his tie and collar and front quite plainly. Again, it disappeared; and we waited a few minutes, then Will (Jr.) spoke. He greeted us both, and said father would speak in a few minutes, and we soon heard father's strong voice, full of emotion, as he greeted us both, and we talked for some time about our life and work, etc. He spoke of the strikes going on in England at the time, etc. and how he would wield his pen still, but was unable. He could go to the office, but no one saw him, or heard him. On Monday, June 7, we had another sitting, and it was at this sitting that father gave us the signal light with which he had invariably signaled his approach at our sittings since.

On June 19, Stead communicated after several other spirits talked with sitters and told his daughter that he felt Edith Harper, his secretary, should be the one to write his biography. Apparently, there had been some prior discussion as to who should write the biography. Stead then greeted Moore and later shouted "Stained Glass." This was particularly evidential to Moore and others as, when he was alive, Stead would good naturedly shout "Stained Glass" when he wanted to abruptly end a conversation because his point was not being grasped. This referred to the distortion in spirit communication as it comes through the medium, something Stead had observed when alive and had likened to looking at a scene through stained glass.

On July 3, Mrs. Wriedt's final séance before returning home, Moore noted that a partial etherealisation of Stead took place – "an illuminated head and some white stuff underneath, but the features were not distinguishable." They were told by Iola, Moore's deceased relative, that it was Stead. William Stead, Jr. again spoke with his sister, Estelle. Moore asked him to give his kindest regards to his father. "He hears you Admiral," Stead Jr. replied.

But Wriedt remained in England for several more weeks and attended a séance at the home of Professor and Mrs. Coates. "On the evening of July 17th, Mr. Stead etherealised twice," Peter Reid an artist and one of the sitters, documented. "The first time in cloudy form – not very clear. The second time, sufficiently defined to be recognized. When Mrs. Coates and others spoke, the head bowed in acknowledgement. Later I heard him address Professor and Mrs. Coates in an earnest and sympathetic voice. There was something optimistic and catching in the tone of that clear voice, and his parting blessing must be remembered by all. There were 14 persons present, including Mrs. Wriedt and myself."

When the *Titanic* went down, Estelle Stead was on a tour with her own Shakespearean Company. One of the members of the touring group was a young man named Pardoe Woodman. According to Estelle, a few days before the disaster, Woodman told her over tea that there was to be a great disaster at sea and that an elderly man very close to her would be among the victims. Five years later, in 1917, shortly after being discharged from the army, Woodman began receiving messages from Stead by means of automatic writing. Estelle observed Woodman in the automatic writing process and noted that he wrote with his eyes closed and that the writing was very much like her father's. Moreover, the writing would stop at times and go back to dot the "i's" and cross the "t's," a habit of her father's which she was sure Woodman knew nothing about.

"Practically instantaneously I found myself looking for myself," Stead told his daughter about his awakening to his death state. "Just a moment of agitation, momentary only, and then the full and glorious realisation that all I had learned was true...I was still so near the earth that I could see everything going on..." Passing to the very end, he related:

The end came and it was all finished with. It was like waiting for a liner to sail; we waited until all were aboard. I mean we waited until the disaster was complete. The saved – saved; the dead – alive. Then in one whole we moved our scene. It was a strange method of traveling for us all, and we were a strange crew, bound for we knew not where. The whole scene was indescribably pathetic. Many, knowing what had occurred, were in agony of doubt as to their people left behind and as to their own future state. What would it hold for them? Would they be taken to see Him? What would their sentence be? Others were almost mental wrecks. They knew nothing, they seemed to be uninterested in everything, their minds were paralysed. A strange crew indeed, of human souls waiting their ratings in the new land.

A matter of a few minutes in time only, and here were hundreds of bodies floating in the water – dead – hundreds of souls carried through the air, alive; very much alive, some were. Many, realizing their death had come, were enraged at their own powerlessness to save their valuables. They fought to save what they had on earth prized so much.

They waited until all souls were collected, Stead continued, and then they seemed to rise vertically into the air at terrific speed, as if they were on a large platform hurled into the air with gigantic speed and strength. Yet, there was no feeling of insecurity. He could not tell how long the journey lasted, but he said that his arrival "was like walking from your own English winter gloom into the radiance of an Indian sky. There was all brightness and beauty. It was all lightness, brightness. Some were still in shock, others not. Those still suffering seemed to be souls who had not believed in a spirit world or had not realized how close it was to the physical world. At that point, they all parted company, though each one seemed to be accompanied by someone who had been on that side for some time.

Stead found himself in company with his father and an old friend. His father told him that he came to show him around. He likened it to arriving in a foreign country with an old friend waiting there to show him around. Stead lost track of time and couldn't tell whether he had "died" 50 years ago or the previous night. He was taken to a temporary "rest house" for newly-arrived spirits. "At first there is nothing done but what is both helpful and comforting – later there is a refining process to be gone through," he explained. At first it is possible to be closely in touch with the home left behind, but after a little time there is a reaction from the desire to be so close to earth, and when that sets in the process of eliminating earth and flesh instincts begins. In each case, this takes a different course, a different length of time."

Because time now had a different meaning for him, he was unable to say how long before he made his first attempt to link up with earth again, but believed it to be a few days in earth time, though it seemed much longer than that to him. He said that he had a helper, or "official," with him on his first attempt to show himself.

Then came the attempt. There were two or three people in this room and they were all talking together about the horror of this great disaster and about the probability of people coming back. They were holding a séance, and my official showed me how to make my presence known. The controlling force, he told me, was thought. I had to visualise myself among these people in the flesh. Imagine I was standing there in the flesh, in the centre of them, and then imagine myself still there with a strong light thrown upon me...Create the picture. Hold the visualization very deliberately and in detail, and keep it fixed upon my mind, that at the moment I was there and that they were conscious of it. I failed, of course, at first, but I know that after a few attempts I succeeded and those people did actually see me. My face only, but that was only because in my picture I had seen myself only as a face. I imagined the part they would recognise me by. I was also able to get a message in the same way. Precisely the same way. I stood by the most sensitive present, and spoke and concentrated my mind on a short sentence, and repeated it with much emphasis and deliberation until I could hear part of it spoken by the person. I knew that at last I had succeeded, and I succeeded reasonably easily because I knew so intimately what the conditions of those people and that earth room were. Many who had not my earth knowledge made little impression.

There were none of my own family present that time. Had there been it would made it impossible for me, as I was then feeling their sorrow acutely, and I would not have been able to give my mind so full a power as I did – I became almost impersonal. It was a good thing that my first attempt was purely a test one – to see if I could break through to home. .

Stead continued, stating that when a person on earth directs his or her thoughts to those on his side, it is as if it is a direct call and they are practically always able to come in contact with the person and impress thoughts and ideas upon the person's mind. "He will seldom accept them for what they are," Stead went on, "but will think they are his own normal thoughts or something of a hallucination. Nevertheless, if frequent opportunity is given he will be startled at the amount of information he can record...Anyone who sits for a moment and allows his mind to dwell on some dear one who had 'died' will actually draw the spirit of that person to himself. He may be conscious or unconscious of the presence, but the presences is there."

Stead stressed that in transitioning to the spirit world one does not immediately become part of the "Godhead," nor does the "spirit" have full knowledge on all subjects. "I cannot tell you when your grandson will next require shoes...nor can I tell you the settlement of the Irish question. I can only see a little farther than you, and I do not by any means possess the key to the door of All Knowledge and All Truth. That, we have each to work for...and as we pass through one door we find another in front of us to be unlocked....and another, and another." He added that as progress is made and earth's inclinations and habits put aside, other interests take their places and then comes the desire for true knowledge.

"Life here is a grander thing – a bolder thing, and a happier thing for all those who have led reasonable lives on earth," Stead further explained, "but for the unreasonable there are many troubles and difficulties and sorrows to be encountered. There is a great truth in the saying that 'as ye sow, so shall ye reap'."

SIX

AFTERLIFE RESCUE
OF A TITANIC VICTIM

*Missionary spirits minister to souls in the Shadowlands. Residents
can free themselves if they are willing to face up humbly to their
errors and crimes and repent them. Some do; and most, perhaps
all, will eventually. But many jeer at their would-be helpers and
seem to prefer their dull lives over the challenges of higher worlds
they are frightened of.*

> – **Stafford Betty,** Ph.D.
> "The Afterlife Unveiled"

Much of the literature dealing with afterlife communication suggests that quite a few souls, or spirits, are, because of materialistic
ways during their earth lives, slow to awaken to their new reality. As
a result, they remain "earthbound," a large percentage of them not
even aware that they are "dead." These were souls who did little or
nothing to develop spiritual consciousness while alive in the flesh.
They were not necessarily evil people, but they failed to develop the
qualities of love, empathy, humility, service, and charity when "alive"
in their earth bodies. After death, they dwell in what has been called
the "Shadowlands," or the "Borderlands," and cling to their earthly
ways in sort of a dream world, sometimes obsessing or possessing
spiritually weak humans. It is as if they are having a nightmare, re-
living those parts of their earth lives in which their selfish ways gov-
erned. This spiritually unconscious state can continue for years in
earth time. It is a "fire of the mind," what religions call hell. However, unlike the hell of orthodoxy, it is not a permanent state. These

earthbound souls can be awakened and slowly evolve to higher states of consciousness.

The earthbound condition is a matter of degree. Those who developed a modicum of spiritual consciousness may exist in something of a stupor, perhaps recognizing, at times at least, that they are dead, but for the most part still living in a dream world. It is as if they are totally absorbed in a movie, feeling the emotion supposedly experienced by the actors at times and at other times reminding themselves that it is just a movie, not real life.

Strangely, many of these earthbound souls, we are told, resist help. They are still so grounded in materialism, still so closed-minded, still too proud to admit the error of their ways, that they reject being rescued, or if a spirit from a higher realm attempts to help them they react in the same way they would have in the earth life The vibration rate of the "missionary spirits," – those who might help the earthbound spirits – is so great in comparison with the vibration rate of the earthbound spirits that the earthbound spirits don't hear them, or don't understand them. It is very similar to a religious missionary on earth going to a country of heathens and trying to convert them to his or her religion.

One of the pioneers of psychical research was French educator Allan Kardec. In his 1868 book, *Heaven and Hell*, Kardec told of a message received though a Le Havre medium on December 8, 1863. A friend came through first, but said he had to step aside in order to let unhappy and suffering spirits come through. "I'm in a horrible abyss! Help me!...O my God! Who will take me out of this whirlpool?" one such vanquished spirit communicated. "Who will lend a helping hand to the miserable wretch who is being sucked in by the sea?...The night is so dark that I am full of terror...Everywhere the roaring of the waves, and no friendly word to console me and to aid me in this fearful hour; for this dark night is death, death in all its horror, and I will not die. O God! It is not coming death, it is death that is past...I am separated for ever from those I love...I see my body; and what I felt a moment ago was only the remembrance of the frightful anguish of the separation..."

The vanquished spirit identified himself as Ferdinand Bertin. It was subsequently determined that Bertin was the victim of a shipwreck off the coast of France on December 2, six days before the message was received. It was reported that Bertin had perished in making superhuman efforts to save the crew of the lost vessel.

"Although his death had taken place several days before, the spirit was still undergoing all its anguish," Kardec analyzed the communication.

"It is evident that he did not understand his own situation. He fancies himself to be still alive and struggling with the waves, and, at the same time, he speaks of his body as though he were separated from it; he shouts for help, and, a moment afterwards, he speaks of the cause of his death, which he recognizes as having been a punishment; all this denotes the confusion of ideas which usually follow violent death."

Kardec wrote that Bertin again communicated two months later, on February 2, 1864. "The pity you showed for my horrible suffering has given me relief," Bertin communicated. "I begin to hope; I look forward to forgiveness, but after the punishment of my crime. I still suffer, and if I am permitted, for a few moments, to foresee the end of my affliction, it is only to the prayers of charitable hearts, who feel for my misery, that I owe this consolation."

Bertin then said that he felt calmer when able to communicate through the medium. "Your prayers do me good; do not refuse them to me! I would fain not fall back into the hideous dream that becomes a reality when I see it."

Several days later, Bertin communicated through another medium. Kardec asked what prompted him to manifest through the first medium. "...I think I must have been led to the medium by a will superior to my own," he replied, adding that he did not understand it. He further said the he had no conception of time. However, he had come to understand that in a previous existence he had been responsible for having several people sewn up in sacks and thrown into the sea. Thus, he saw his present anguish, which was continuing although not as severe, as punishment for that act.

William T. Stead may have been just such a "superior will" involved in missionary work on the other side, rescuing earthbound spirits, and bringing a *Titanic* victim to the home of Carl A. Wickland, M.D., a psychiatrist who specialized in helping such spirits "go into the light." A member of the Chicago Medical Society and the American Association for the Advancement of Science, Wickland discovered that many cases of mental illness were the result of obsessing or possessing spirits – earthbound or vagabond spirits who attached themselves to living individuals and influenced them in negative ways, including schizophrenia, paranoia, depression, addiction, manic-depression, criminal behavior and phobias of all kind.

"Spirit obsession is a fact – a perversion of a natural law – and is amply demonstrable," Wickland wrote in his 1924 book, *Thirty Years Among the Dead*. "This has been proven hundreds of times by causing the supposed insanity or aberration to be temporarily transferred from the victim to a psychic sensitive who is trained for the purpose, and by this method ascertain the cause of the psychosis to be an ignorant or mischievous spirit, whose identity may frequently be verified."

Born in Sweden, Wickland came to the United States in 1881, married Anna W. Anderson in 1896 and graduated from Durham Medical College in 1900. He became chief psychiatrist at the National Psychopathic Institute of Chicago in 1909 and left that position in 1918 to establish the National Psychological Institute of Los Angeles.

Wickland's wife, Anna, was a trance medium. Their method of combating the vagabond spirits attached to Wickland's patients was to administer an electrical charge to the patient and drive the obsessing spirits from the patient to Mrs. Wickland. These obsessing spirits would then talk to Dr. Wickland using Anna Wickland's body. Nearly all of them didn't know they were "dead" and so Wickland explained their plight to them.

Mrs. Wickland was said to be protected from the vagabond spirits remaining with her by a group of strong intelligences known as "The Mercy Band." As a representative of this Mercy band explained to Wickland, these earthbound entities become attracted to certain humans and attach themselves to the human aura, unwittingly conveying their thoughts to these individuals. It was further explained that the earthbound spirits could not be helped by spirits on their side until they recognized they were "dead."

With one patient, Wickland related, he conversed with 21 different spirits through his wife. In all, they spoke six different languages even though Anna Wickland spoke only Swedish and English.

In *Thirty Years*, Wickland sets forth numerous cases of spirit release dislodgement, including the dialogue that went on between him and the vagabond spirits attached to his patients. As an example, with a patient identified only as "Miss R.F." a spirit calling himself Edward Sterling began speaking through Mrs. Wickland's vocal cords. At first, he didn't remember his last name and couldn't remember what town he was from although he knew he was born in Iowa. When asked what year it was, Edward said it was 1901 (the year he had died). Wickland informed him that it was now 1920. Edward struggled to understand why his hair was now long and he had on women's clothes. Wickland explained to him that he was now "dead" and occupying his wife's (Mrs. Wickland's) body. "If I was dead I would go to the grave and stay there until the last day," Edward responded. "You stay there until Gabriel blows the horn."

At the end of a long conversation, Wickland seems to have convinced Sterling that his physical body had died, but that his spirit body was very much alive and that he should detach himself from Miss R.F. and let her get on with her own life. Wickland noted people take their beliefs with them when they die and that the false teachings of religion often keep them earthbound.

With a patient referred to as "Mrs. R.," a spirit named Ralph Stevenson took over Mrs. Wickland's body and began speaking to Dr. Wickland. Stevenson said he was "straggling along" when he saw a "light," so he came in. However, he couldn't figure out who he was or where he was. He thought it was 1902, when, in fact, it was 1919. When Wickland asked him how long he had been dead, Stevenson replied: "Dead, you say? Why I'm not dead; I wish I were." Wickland asked him why he preferred to be dead and Stevenson said things had been very unpleasant for him. "If I am dead, then it is very hard to be dead," he said. "I have tried and tried to die, but it seems every single time I come to life again. Why is it that I cannot die?"

Stevenson went on to say that he often thinks he is dead, but then he is alive again. "Sometimes I get in places (auras) but I am always pushed out in the dark again, and I go from place to place. I cannot find my home and I cannot die." Wickland noted that Mrs. R., his patient, had often talked about killing herself. Further conversation with Stevenson revealed that he and a young woman named Alice were engaged to be married. However, when her parents objected to the marriage, he decided to kill Alice and himself. After killing Alice, he said he could not kill himself. In fact, he did succeed in killing himself after shooting Alice, but he assumed that he had failed and had been on the run ever since.

After Wickland convinced him that he, in fact, had succeeded in killing himself, Stevenson recognized his mother (in spirit). The mother then took over Mrs. Wickland's body and explained that she had been trying to get through to her son for a long time, but he had built up a barrier that she could not penetrate until now. "He ran away from me whenever he saw me, and neither Alice nor I could come near him," the mother communicated. "He thought he was alive and that he had not killed himself. Some time ago he came in contact with a sensitive person, a woman (Mrs. R), and has been obsessing her, but he thought he was in prison."

Another of Wickland's patients was a pharmacist with a drug addiction problem, especially addicted to morphine. After the patient was administered an electrical shock, the obsessing spirit jumped into Mrs. Wickland's entranced body. Mrs. Wickland's body then began violently coughing. Dr. Wickland asked what the problem was and the spirit replied that she was dying and needed some morphine. Wickland explained to her that she was already dead, but the spirit ignored his comments and continued to beg for morphine.

Wickland managed to calm her down enough to further explain the situation to her and ask her for a name. At first she couldn't remember, but after several moments of searching gave her name as Elizabeth Noble. She said that she was 42 years old and was living in El Paso, Texas. After again begging for morphine, she noticed her husband, Frankie, standing there (in spirit). Frank Noble then took over Mrs. Wickland's body and explained to Wickland that he had died before his wife and had been trying to get her to realize she had "passed out," but had been unsuccessful. He thanked Wickland for explaining the situation to her and said that she would now understand and be better.

But not all earthbound or vagabond spirits attach themselves to humans. Some just flounder in the "ethers" until a missionary spirit can get through to them. William T. Stead was doing some missionary work on the other side and brought a spirit identified only as "John J. A." to Wickland. Only one *Titanic* passenger fits those initials, John Jacob Astor, a first-class passenger who was believed to be the richest man in the world at the time. Wickland wrote that the spirit came in, struggling desperately, as if swimming (his wife's motions), and called for aid. The following dialogue was recorded:

> Wickland: Where did you come from?
>
> John J.A.: That man who just left told me to come in here.
>
> Wickland: Have you been in the water?
>
> John J.A.: I drowned, but I have come to life again. I cannot see that man now, but I heard him talking and he told me to step in. He said that you know the way and would teach me, and that I could go with him afterwards. But now I cannot see him. I'm blind! I'm blind! I don't know whether the water blinded me or not, but I am blind.
>
> Wickland: That is only spiritual blindness. When a person passes out of his physical body without knowledge of the laws of the higher life, he finds himself in a condition of darkness. It is the darkness of ignorance.
>
> John J.A.: Then I will not always be blind?

Wickland: You must realize that you are in the spirit world and that spirit friends are here who will teach you how to progress out of your condition of darkness.

John J.A.: I can see a little now. For a while I could see, but the door was shut again and I could not see through. I was with my wife and child for a time, but no one noticed me. But now the door is closed and I am out in the cold. I am all alone when I go to my home. Changes seem to have taken place. I do not know what I shall do.

Wickland: You have not realized your own situation.

John J.A.: What is the matter anyway? What is causing this darkness? What can I do to get out of it? I never was so handicapped as I am now. I was all right for just a minute. I hear somebody talking. There, now I see him again. Was it Mr. Stead?

Wickland: Mr. Stead was speaking through this instrument just before you came. Mr. Stead probably brought you here for help. It is our work to awaken earthbound spirits who are in darkness.

John J.A.: This darkness is terrible. I have been in this darkness for a long time.

Wickland: Understand that there is no death. Life continues in the spirit world, where each one must serve others in order to progress.

John J.A. I really was not what I should have been. I just lived for self. I wanted amusement and to spend money. But now all I have seen is my past, and I have been in the darkness, and it is terrible. Every act of my past stands before me, and I want to run away from it, but I cannot. It is there all the time and accuses me, because I could have done it differently. I have seen so many places where I could have done good, but now it seems too late.

Wickland: When a person lives for self alone he usually finds himself in darkness when he passes over to the other side of life. You must obtain understanding of the glories of the spirit world and realize that life there is service to others. That is the true "Heaven" – it is a condition of mind.

John J.A. Why are not these things taught in the world?

Wickland: Would the world listen? Humanity as a whole does not look for the spiritual side of life, but looks for other things. The world is seeking an amusement for selfish gain, not for truth.

John J.A.: There is such a queer feeling coming over me. Mother! Mother, my loving mother! I am a man, but I feel like a child in your arms again. I have been longing for you, but I have been living all by myself in the terrible darkness. Why is it that I should be in the dark? Cannot my eyes be cured? Will I be blind all the time? Isn't it strange that I should see you, yet I seem to be blind?

Wickland: You have a spiritual body now, and when your spiritual eyes are opened you will see the beautiful things of the spirit world.

John J.A. I see Mr. Stead there. We were both on the same boat, but he does not seem to be in the dark.

Wickland: He understood the truth of spirit return and life on the other side while he was on earth. Life is a school and we must learn all we can about the spirit side of life while we are on earth, for the only light we have when we pass to the other side is the knowledge pertaining to life's problems which we have gathered here.

John J.A.: Why did no one ever tell me these things?

Wickland: Would you have listened to any one who would have tried to talk to you on these subjects?

John J.A. No one ever approached me with such ideas.

Wickland: What year do you think this is?

John J.A.: 1912

Wickland: It is 1916.

John J.A. Where have I been? I have been very hungry and cold. I had a very great deal of money, but lately when I have wanted some to spend I could not get hold of it. Sometimes I seemed to be shut up in a room very dark, and I could see nothing but a procession of my past life. I was not a bad man, but you probably know what society people are. I did not know until now what it was to be poor. It is a new experience to me. Why should humanity not be taught differently before death? Then there would not be such suffering as I am in now.

Wickland: If you will go with your mother and other spirit friends and try to understand what they tell you, you will feel much happier.

John J.A.: I can see Mr. Stead. I met him on the boat but I had no use for his teachings. I thought he was old and that he had a hobby. You know when people get old they have hobbies of one kind or another. I never had time for such things, because all I thought of was my money and society. We do not see the poor people and we do not care to see them. I could do so differently now, but money is of no use to me any longer. My mother is waiting for me and I should like to go with her, for I have not seen her for years, and it is so good to see her. She says she could not reach me, for I was like a crazy man and would not listen to her. Bless you all for the help you have been to me, and for having opened my eyes. It is misery to be blind, yet able to see the procession of your past life and not be able to see or hear anything else.

Wickland: We should like to know your name.

John J.A.: I am John J. A., and I am glad I met you all. I am so grateful for what you have told me. Now I can see and hear, and understand something that I did not know existed. My mother and friends are coming for me, and now I am going through that beautiful gate into what will be to me Heaven. I again thank you all, and hope some day to come and see you again. Goodbye.

On November 5, 1916, John J.A. returned to the Wickland home, bringing a friend identified by Wickland only as "Alfred V." but obviously Alfred Vanderbilt, who was a victim of the sinking of the *Lusitania* by a German submarine on May 7, 1915. The dialogue was again recorded:

Alfred V.: Somebody told me to come in here and I would get warm.

Wickland: What is your name?

Alfred V.: Alfred V. I was on a boat. John J.A. came and told me he would try to help me get in here. He said if I would come in here I would get help. Say, I have never been hungry in my life before, but I am both hungry and cold, as my clothes are all wet.

Wickland: That is only a condition of your mind. You have lost your physical body and should not feel the need of food.

Alfred V. I know I drowned and I have been in misery ever since.

Wickland: If you had an understanding of the life hereafter and of progression in the spirit world you would soon find happiness through serving others.

Alfred V. I never was happy. I suppose I had my own way too

much, yet sometimes I felt, what was the use. But I thought: "Just forget yourself and have a good time." You may not care for society life, but in society you can drown yourself in gaiety. I really did not care for society life. I used to forget myself with horses. If you have a beautiful horse he is faithful to you through life. But when you get into society, women just show you one side – smiles, and sometimes they hate you. The love I know most is the love of a beautiful, faithful horse. Horses were my pleasure and I felt they loved me. Women liked me only for what I could do for them. They wanted money and pleasure. Women wanted all the money they could get from me. I let go of things and tried to lose myself in pleasure, but I was not happy. Society does not know anything about honor and respectability. If I could find people as faithful and true as my horse was to me, I tell you I would thank you for that society. But go into the kind of society I have known, and men and women are nothing. I was a sport myself, but there were things that drove me to forget that little think within me, conscience. I longed for something that was good, but where can you find it? Not amongst society, but amongst horses. Society is all right if you want that kind of life. You will probably realize that I developed a great deal of selfishness.

Wickland: You must try now to forget your past life with all its sorrow and bitterness. Look for higher things; then your spiritual eyes will be opened.

Alfred V. Friends that took an interest in me brought me here, and my eyes have been opened since I came. I feel that probably – but I am not sure – a time may come when I can be happy. I have never been really happy, for when a child I had my own way too much. I thank you for allowing me to come here. If I ever am truly happy I will come back and tell you so.

Wickland recorded that both John J.A. and Alfred V. returned several years later, bringing a friend, Anna H., who had been a stage celebrity in earth life. Like both John J.A. and Alfred V. were at the time of first visiting the Wicklands, Anna H. was in a state of extreme confusion and did not realize she had died. She found it difficult to understand how both John and Alfred could be talking to her when she knew that both were dead. Dr. Wickland asked her if she knew where her two friends were. "I do not like the name, but they say, 'The Spirit World,' Anna replied. "They say that it is the home beyond the grave.

They say I shall have to overcome my earthly conditions before I can open my psychic eyes. I do not know what they mean."

Anna lamented the loss of her beauty. "Life was very sweet while I had admirers," she continued. "But I suffered for my vanity. The doctors said if I had not laced so much I would not have been so sick. I would not mind the doctors either. They wanted me to eat to get strength, but I was afraid if I lay there and ate, and did not get my regular massage and baths, I could not keep my form, so I starved myself. When I was in the dark, Alfred came to me and said: 'Come – I will show you something far more beautiful than a beautiful form and selfishness and vanity. They are only shadows. Now come, and we will show you why we should live for others. You will be beautiful again when you have served others, but you must forget self and overcome all selfishness." With the help of the Wicklands, Anna H. was able to "see the light" and go into it.

While mainstream medicine and science scoffed then and continue to scoff at such "ridiculous" ideas as spirit influence and spirit rescue, there are a growing number of enlightened physicians and mental health therapists who see the wisdom in the research and practices advanced by such pioneers as Kardec and Wickland. "From the Spiritist point of view, after ruling out physical brain damage or disabilities such as retardation, the cause of most mental illness is embedded in the perispirit, also known today as the 'informational body' or 'subtle body,' states Emma Bragdon, Ph.D., who has been studying Spiritistic healing in Brazil for eleven years and is the editor of *Spiritism and Mental Health*, published in 2011. The book offers testimonies of 30 psychiatrists, psychologists, physicians and therapists, including a number of Americans, who subscribe to spirit healing.

Spiritism, the philosophy developed by Kardec, is designed to bring together science, parapsychology, and healing, and is especially popular in Brazil, where an estimated 20 percent of Brazil's 200-million population are served by more than 12,000 Spiritist community centers and 50 Spiritist psychiatric hospitals. The Spiritist psychiatric hospitals, Bragdon says, integrate the best of medical technology with the best of complementary care, with a strong spiritual base. While the primary aim of the treatment is to free living humans of obsession by obsessing spirits, the obsessing spirit is also helped in the process by coming to understand "its" earthbound condition and freeing "itself" of it.

"Spiritism does not deny the bio-psycho-social causes of mental disorders," Alexander Moreira-Almeida, M.D., Ph.D., states in one of the two chapters he contributed to Bragdon's book. "It fully acknowledges them. Kardec always emphasized that Spiritism does not come to deny well-established scientific knowledge; it comes to complement it, adding something new – the spiritual element – to our understanding of nature. Several times he compared Spiritism with microbiology; both reveal and investigate dimensions of reality that are invisible to the naked eye but are part of the natural world and can affect our lives."

By putting "Spirit Rescue" into a search engine, the reader will find evidence of much activity in this area today. The fact that both mainstream science and orthodox religion do not recognize it is by no means evidence of its unreality. "The unscientific attitude and aloofness of the medical fraternity toward any research that suggests discarnated spirits, due to fear of ostracism, of jeopardizing professional standing, or owing to the fallacious notion that it is unethical and beneath the dignity of science to follow such research, is today a serious obstacle to advancement of knowledge pertaining to contributing causes underlying mental aberrations and insanity," he wrote in his second book, *The Gateway of Understanding*, "and is a hindrance to neurological and psychiatric research."

Mediumship Then & Now

We cannot begin to live fully until we come to terms with the reality of death. We cannot know true courage until we look death in the face and see that it is not a voracious monster with yawning jaws that will eventually gobble up everything we hold precious, but instead a thing of beauty and wonder and great adventure.
– Lily Fairchilde
"Voices from the Afterlife"

At the time the *Titanic* went down, in 1912, spiritualism, as spirit communication through mediums came to be called, was still pretty much in its heyday, although perhaps not quite as popular as it had been during the second half of the nineteenth century. It had had its advent in 1848 with the so-called "Rochester Knockings" in New York, when the Fox sisters of Hydesville, a hamlet of Rochester, figured out that there was an "intelligence" behind the loud raps and knocks they heard on their walls. They began communicating with the "intelligence," said to be a former resident of the house who had been murdered and buried under the house. The earliest form of mediumship involved so many raps for each letter of the alphabet and one rap for "no" and three for "yes."

It was soon realized that the Fox sisters were mediums and were able to bring through other spirits. Some amazing phenomena produced by their spirit "controls" (the spirits assisting them) were witnessed by a number of eminent men and women, including Horace Greeley, J. Fenimore Cooper, and William Cullen Bryant. Word of the

Fox family phenomena quickly spread around the United States and then to England, France, and other parts of Europe, and mediumship soon flourished. It became increasingly clear that the "spirits" could use only certain people in their efforts to communicate. These people, who apparently had a higher rate of vibration than most, were called "mediums" as they served as "go-betweens" in relaying messages to those sitting with the mediums.

From raps and taps, spiritualism went to table tipping (one tip of the table being like a rap) and then to physical mediumship, including levitations and materializations, and to other forms of mediumship, such as automatic writing, trance-speaking, and the direct-voice. The latter, the form of mediumship employed by Etta Wriedt, as discussed in Chapter 5, was considered by most researchers to be the most evidential, But it apparently was the most difficult as there were very few direct-voice mediums.

One of the earliest investigators of the phenomena was Professor Robert Hare, a University of Pennsylvania chemist and inventor. Hare set out to debunk all mediumship, but soon became a believer. In fact, he developed into a medium himself. In one sitting, Hare asked his deceased father what the mediumship epidemic was all about, and was told that it was "a deliberate effort on the part of the inhabitants of the higher spheres to break through the partition which has interfered with the attainment, by mortals, of a correct idea of their destiny after death." To carry out this intention, a delegation of advanced spirits had been appointed, Hare was told. This came at a time when materialism was beginning to thrive and the educated were abandoning their religions. Thus, these advanced spirits felt something was needed to curb the tide and restore a belief in God and in life after death.

Besides Hare, a number of other prominent scholars and scientists investigated mediums and also became believers. It was not until 1882, however, that a group of scientists and scholars in England organized the Society for Psychical Research (SPR) in order to conduct more formal investigations of mediums, employing strict scientific controls. Three years later, the American branch of the SPR was formed, spearheaded by Harvard psychologist William James. While the early investigators uncovered much fraud in the area, with people trying to pose as mediums and make money from it, they also came to recognize that there were genuine mediums. They debated, however, whether the information coming through mediums was from spirits or from the subconscious of the individuals, combined with telepathy, or mind-reading. When information came through that was unknown to the medium and the person sitting with the medium, the researchers wondered if mediums had the ability to read minds anywhere in the world or to tap into some cosmic reservoir for information. As both telepathy and the cosmic reservoir theories were as opposed to mechanistic theories of the universe as spirits were, the majority of educated men refused to accept even those theories, or hypotheses.

Three schools of thought emerged: 1) one accepting spirits and spirit communication; 2) one believing the phenomena were all a function of the subconscious; and, 3) one certain it was all fraudulent. The vast majority of scientists and educated men and women were in the latter two schools, as it was simply not "intelligent" to believe in spirits. After all, science was trying to rid the world of religious superstitions.

Even though there were a number of very distinguished scientists who had investigated mediumship and spoke out in favor of spirits, they were in the minority and their reputations suffered. The majority of scientists and scholars, though they had not themselves investigated mediumship, assumed that their brethren who had investigated were simply victims of good magicians. Moreover, some legitimate mediums, including the Fox sisters, apparently turned to fraudulent methods when their powers failed them. They were expected to perform, and if nothing happened, they made it happen by trickery so that those viewing would not be disappointed. These so-called "mixed mediums" – producing genuine phenomena at times and fraudulent at other times – only served to discredit the honest mediums.

Meanwhile, orthodox religion also opposed spiritualism, as some of the teachings of the spirits conflicted with the dogma and doctrines of the churches. Thus, the churches called it all demonic.

Because there was so much resistance and fraud, spiritualism began to decline somewhat during the 1890s and the first decade of the 20th Century. World War I brought about a revival, as people wanted to hear from their loved ones killed in the war. But after the war, spiritualism again began to decline and never recovered.

While skeptics claim that the decline was the result of more strict controls in the investigations, spiritualists claimed that many of the best mediums refused to be studied or tested because the researchers did not understand the phenomena and were intent on exposing good mediums as frauds, thereby seriously damaging their reputations. Indeed it appears clear that a number of genuine mediums were defamed by the SPR and other research organizations because they expected the spirits to perform in ways that they could understand. When they couldn't understand it, they judged it fraud.

At the same time, academia had bought into the materialistic paradigm and refused to have anything to do with psychical research, as it was called. Researchers began calling themselves parapsychologists and concerning themselves with paranormal phenomena not directly related to spirits and the afterlife, such as telepathy, psychokinesis, and precognition. While finding evidence for various phenomena, these parapsychologists deemed it much more academically acceptable to justify their findings by attributing them to the subconscious, generally not even mentioning a spiritual cause.

Another reason often cited for the decline in mediumship is the lack of quiet time brought about by radio, television, and other entertainment. Generally, mediumship requires a passive attitude and development, much like meditation, and technological advances resulted in fewer opportunities to sit quietly in one's home and discover his or her inner nature. And as people socialized less, due to the home entertainment, mediumship circles, which fostered certain types of phenomena, declined.

But there were also indications that those advanced spirits abandoned their efforts because it had reached a point of diminishing returns. William Stainton Moses, one of the most credible and best mediums of the early era, was told by his spirit "control" that they (the spirits) had misjudged man's ability to be enlightened in this way. They did not anticipate so much resistance, nor did they anticipate so much interference from low-level spirits. These low-level spirits were closer in vibration to the physical world and so could easily block and distort messages from higher realms.

When people today think of mediumship, they assume it is all of the clairvoyant and clairaudient type, as witnessed in some television programs. While such mediumship can be evidential, it is hardly as dynamic and impressive as that demonstrated by Etta Wriedt, Anna Wickland, Jessie Coates, and others mentioned in this book.

The mediumship of 80-160 years ago, while varying in types and degrees, produced both evidence of survival and enlightenment, at least for those open-minded and discerning enough to study the volumes of material. The key messages, those which *Titanic* victim William T. Stead came to understand are:

- The world is a non-mechanistic one, controlled by a higher form of consciousness than that possessed by humans.

- Death is merely a transition to another realm of existence.

- We cross over to the Other Side much the same as we leave the earth realm.

- The Other Side is made up of many realms, planes, spheres, or levels, and we gravitate to the realm we have earned in this lifetime based on what has been called a "moral specific gravity."

- It is possible for spirits to communicate with the earth realm through human instruments referred to as mediums. These mediums are not necessarily saintly individuals, but do have a higher rate of vibration than most humans.

- There is often much distortion in the messages coming from the spirit world due to the fact that the communication often comes by thought visualizations and must be interpreted by the medium's brain. (This is not necessarily so with the direct-voice phenomenon.)

- Most spirits are not able to communicate directly and require a "control" on their side to pass on messages to or through the medium. This process also results in confusion and distortion of the messages.

- Earthbound spirits often attach themselves to humans and influence the behavior of the human.

- Earthbound and other low-level spirits are often mischievous and can represent themselves as famous people or as deceased loved ones. Thus, it is necessary to "test" the messages "whether they are of God."

- The earthbound of low-level spirits may experience a "fire of the mind," what religions call "hell," but this is not a permanent state. With help and understanding, these low-level spirits can "see the light" and progress to a higher realm.

- Earth life is intended as a school in which we can learn and progress faster than by remaining in the spirit world.

- The "real" world is the one we transition to when we die.

- Preparing for death helps us better enjoy this life and more quickly adapt and adjust to the next life.

Bibliography

Bates, E. Katharine Bates, *Seen and Unseen*, Dodge Publishing Co., New York, 1908

Becker, Ernest, *The Denial of Death*, Simon & Schuster, NY, 1973

Betty, Stafford, *The Afterlife Unveiled*, O Books, Winchester, UK, 2011-12-11

Beesley, Lawrence, *The Loss of the S. S. Titanic: Its Story and Its Lessons,* Lawrence Beesley, 1912

Beichler, James E., *To Die For,* Trafford Publishing, Victoria, B.C., 2008

Bragdon, Emma, *Spiritism and Mental Health*, Jessica Kingsley Publishers, 2011

Coates, James, *Has W. T. Stead Returned?*, L. N. Fowler & Co., London, 1913

Crookall, Robert, *Out of the Body Experiences*, Carol Publishing Group, New York, NY, 1992

Delanne, Gabriel, *Evidence for a Future Life*, G. P. Putnam's Sons, New York, 1904

De Montaigne, Michel, *The Complete Essays*, Penguin Books, New York, 1987

Fenwick, Peter & Elizabeth, *The Art of Dying*, Continuum, New York, NY, 2008

Fairchilde, Lily, *Voices from the Afterlife*, St. Martin's Griffin, New York, NY, 1998

Flammarion, Camille, *Death and Its Mystery: Before Death*, T. Fisher Unwin, Ltd., London, 1922

Flammarion, Camille, *Death and Its Mystery: At the Moment of Death*, T. Fisher Unwin, Ltd., 1922

Frankl, Viktor, E., *Man's Search for Meaning*, Washington Square Press, New York, 1959

Gracie, Archibald, *The Truth About the Titanic*, Mitchell Kennerley, 1913

Gurney, Edmund, Myers, F. W. H., Podmore, Frank, *Phantasms of the Living*, Kegan Paul, Trench, Trubner & Co., Ltd., New York, 1918

Harper, Edith H., *Stead, The Man: Personal Reminiscences*, William Rider & Son., Ltd., London, 1918

Harper, Leslie Vernet, *The Secret Conan Doyle Correspondences*, Hascom Publishers, Provo, UT, 1986

Holms, A. Campbell, *The Facts of Psychic Science*, University Books, New Hyde Park, NY, 1969

Jung, C. G., *Memories, Dreams, Reflections*, Vintage Books, NY, 1961

Kardec, Allan, *The Spirits' Book*, White Crow Books, Guildford, England, 2010, (original publication in 1857)

Kierkegaard, S., *Fear and Trembling*, Doubleday & Co., Garden City, NY, 1954

King, John, S. *Dawn of the Awakened Mind*, The James A. McCann Co., New York, 1920

Kingsford, S. M., *Psychical Research for the Plain Man*, Kegan Paul, Trench, Trubner & Co. Ltd. New York, 1920,

Kubler-Ross, Elisabeth, *On Life After Death*, Celestial Arts, Berkeley, Calif.

Lord, Walter, *A Night to Remember*, Henry Holt & Co., New York, 1955

Maeterlinck, Maurice, *Our Eternity*, Dodd, Mead, and Company, New York, NY, 1913

McEneaney, Bonnie, *Messages*, HarperCollins Books, New York, 2010

Mowbray, Jay Henry, *Sinking of the Titanic*, The Minister Co., Harrisburg, PA., 1912

Muldoon, Sylvan & Carrington, Hereward, *The Projection of The Astral Body*, Samuel Weiser, Inc., York Beach, Maine, 1969

Myers, F. W. H., *Human Personality and its Survival of Bodily Death*, University Books, Inc., New Hyde Park, NY, 1961 (reprint of 1903 book)

Osis, Karlis and Haraldsson, Erlendur, *At the Hour of Death*, Avon Books, New York, 1977

Powell, A. E., *The Astral Body*, Quest Books, Wheaton, IL, 1972.

Richet, Charles and DeBrath, Stanley, *Thirty Years of Psychical Research*, W. Collins Son & Co., Ltd., Glascow, 1923

Rinpoche, Sogyal, *The Tibetan Book of Living and Dying*, Harper, San Francisco,1994

Sculthorp, Frederick C., *Excursions to the Spirit World*, The Greater World Association, London, 1961

Shneidman, Edwin S., *Deaths of Man*, Penguin Books, Inc., Baltimore, 1974

Singh, Kathleen Dowling, *The Grace in Dying*, Harper Collins, San Francisco, CA, 1998

Stead, William T., *After Death or Letters from Julia*, The Progressive Thinker Publishing House, 1909, (reprinted by Kessinger Publishing, LLC)

Stead, William T., *How I Know That The Dead Return*, The Ball Publishing Co., Boston, 1909

Stead, W. T., *Borderland*, University Books, New Hyde Park, NY., 1970

Stead, Estelle, *My Father, Personal*, George H. Doran Co., New York, 1913

Stead, Estelle, *The Blue Island*, Hutchinson & Co., London, 1922

Tolstoy, Leo, *A Confession*, White Crow Books, Guildford, England, 2009 (original publication in 1924)

Travers Smith, Hester, *Voices from the Void*, E. P. Dutton & Company, New York, 1919

Turvey, Vincent N., *The Beginnings of Seership*, University Books, Inc., New Hyde Park, N. Y., 1969

Tweedale, Charles L., *Man's Survival After Death*, Psychic book Club, London, 1925

Tymn, Michael, *The Afterlife Revealed*, White Crow Books, Guildford, England, 2011

Whiting, Lilian, *The Spiritual Significance*, Little, Brown, & Co., Boston, 1901

Wickland, Carl A., *Thirty Years Among the Dead*, White Crow Books, Guildford, England, 2011 (original publication in 1924)

Wickland, Carl A., *The Gateway of Understanding*, Health Research, Pomeroy, WA, 1972

Winocour, Jack, *The Story of The Titanic*, Dover Publications, Inc. New York, 1960

http://www.encyclopedia-titanica.org/

http://www.titanic1.org/

Paperbacks also available from
White Crow Books

Marcus Aurelius—*Meditations*
ISBN 978-1-907355-20-2

Elsa Barker—*Letters from
a Living Dead Man*
ISBN 978-1-907355-83-7

Elsa Barker—*War Letters
from the Living Dead Man*
ISBN 978-1-907355-85-1

Elsa Barker—*Last Letters
from the Living Dead Man*
ISBN 978-1-907355-87-5

Richard Maurice Bucke—
Cosmic Consciousness
ISBN 978-1-907355-10-3

G. K. Chesterton—*Heretics*
ISBN 978-1-907355-02-8

G. K. Chesterton—*Orthodoxy*
ISBN 978-1-907355-01-1

Arthur Conan Doyle—*The
Edge of the Unknown*
ISBN 978-1-907355-14-1

Arthur Conan Doyle—
The New Revelation
ISBN 978-1-907355-12-7

Arthur Conan Doyle—
The Vital Message
ISBN 978-1-907355-13-4

Arthur Conan Doyle with
Simon Parke—*Conversations
with Arthur Conan Doyle*
ISBN 978-1-907355-80-6

Meister Eckhart with Simon Parke—
Conversations with Meister Eckhart
ISBN 978-1-907355-18-9

Kahlil Gibran—*The Forerunner*
ISBN 978-1-907355-06-6

Kahlil Gibran—*The Madman*
ISBN 978-1-907355-05-9

Kahlil Gibran—*The Prophet*
ISBN 978-1-907355-04-2

Kahlil Gibran—*Jesus the Son of Man*
ISBN 978-1-907355-08-0

Kahlil Gibran—*Spiritual World*
ISBN 978-1-907355-09-7

D. D. Home—*Incidents
in my Life Part 1*
ISBN 978-1-907355-15-8

Mme. Dunglas Home; edited,
with an Introduction, by Sir
Arthur Conan Doyle—*D. D.
Home: His Life and Mission*
ISBN 978-1-907355-16-5

Edward C. Randall—
Frontiers of the Afterlife
ISBN 978-1-907355-30-1

Lucius Annaeus Seneca—
On Benefits
ISBN 978-1-907355-19-6

Rebecca Ruter Springer—*Intra
Muros: My Dream of Heaven*
ISBN 978-1-907355-11-0

Leo Tolstoy, edited by Simon
Parke—*Forbidden Words*
ISBN 978-1-907355-00-4

Leo Tolstoy—*A Confession*
ISBN 978-1-907355-24-0

Leo Tolstoy—*The Gospel in Brief*
ISBN 978-1-907355-22-6

Leo Tolstoy—*The Kingdom
of God is Within You*
ISBN 978-1-907355-27-1

Leo Tolstoy—*My Religion:
What I Believe*
ISBN 978-1-907355-23-3

Leo Tolstoy—*On Life*
ISBN 978-1-907355-91-2

Leo Tolstoy—*Twenty-three Tales*
ISBN 978-1-907355-29-5

Leo Tolstoy—*What is Religion
and other writings*
ISBN 978-1-907355-28-8

Leo Tolstoy—*Work While
Ye Have the Light*
ISBN 978-1-907355-26-4

Leo Tolstoy with Simon Parke—
Conversations with Tolstoy
ISBN 978-1-907355-25-7

Vincent Van Gogh with
Simon Parke—*Conversations
with Van Gogh*
ISBN 978-1-907355-95-0

Howard Williams with an
Introduction by Leo Tolstoy—*The
Ethics of Diet: An Anthology
of Vegetarian Thought*
ISBN 978-1-907355-21-9

Allan Kardec—*The Spirits Book*
ISBN 978-1-907355-98-1

Wolfgang Amadeus Mozart
with Simon Parke—
Conversations with Mozart
ISBN 978-1-907661-38-9

Jesus of Nazareth with
Simon Parke—*Conversations
with Jesus of Nazareth*
ISBN 978-1-907661-41-9

Thomas à Kempis with Simon
Parke—*The Imitation of Christ*
ISBN 978-1-907661-58-7

Emanuel Swedenborg—
Heaven and Hell
ISBN 978-1-907661-55-6

P.D. Ouspensky—*Tertium Organum:
The Third Canon of Thought*
ISBN 978-1-907661-47-1

Dwight Goddard—*A Buddhist Bible*
ISBN 978-1-907661-44-0

Leo Tolstoy—*The Death
of Ivan Ilyich*
ISBN 978-1-907661-10-5

Leo Tolstoy—*Resurrection*
ISBN 978-1-907661-09-9

Michael Tymn—*The
Afterlife Revealed*
ISBN 978-1-970661-90-7

Guy L. Playfair—*If This Be Magic*
ISBN 978-1-907661-84-6

Julian of Norwich with
Simon Parke—*Revelations of
Divine Love*
ISBN 978-1-907661-88-4

Maurice Nicoll—*The New Man*
ISBN 978-1-907661-86-0

Carl Wickland, M.D.—*Thirty Years
Among the Dead*
ISBN 978-1-907661-72-3

Allan Kardec—*The
Book on Mediums*
ISBN 978-1-907661-75-4

John E. Mack—*Passport
to the Cosmos*
ISBN 978-1-907661-81-5

**All titles available as eBooks, and selected titles available in Hardback and
Audiobook formats from www.whitecrowbooks.com**

CPSIA information can be obtained at www.ICGtesting.com
Printed in the USA
BVOW021954030713

324993BV00003B/677/P